A
BOOK
OF
PAGAN
PRAYER

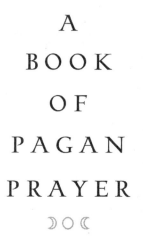

A
BOOK
OF
PAGAN
PRAYER

☽ ○ ☾

CEISIWR SERITH

WEISER BOOKS

First published in 2018 by
Red Wheel/Weiser, LLC
With offices at:
65 Parker Street, Suite 7
Newburyport, MA 01950
www.redwheelweiser.com

ISBN: 978-1-57863-649-5

Names: Serith, Ceisiwr, 1957- author.
Title: A book of pagan prayer / Ceisiwr Serith.
Description: Newburyport : Weiser Books, 2018. | Originally published: 2002.
 | Includes bibliographical references and index.
Identifiers: LCCN 2018035607 | ISBN 9781578636495 (5 x 7 pbk. : alk. paper)
Subjects: LCSH: Prayers. | Witchcraft. | Neopaganism--Prayers and devotions.
Classification: LCC BF1572.P73 S47 2018 | DDC 299/.94--dc23
LC record available at https://lccn.loc.gov/2018035607

Cover design by Kathryn Sky-Peck
Interior black sun graphic by Ratatosk, dist. under CCA-Share Alike 2.0
Interior by Steve Amarillo / Urban Design LLC
Typeset in Ascender Tinos and Emigre Mrs. Eaves

Printed in Canada
MAR
11 10 9 8 7 6 5

For Phyllis R. Huggett
who told me I was smart

☽ ○ ☾

CONTENTS

PREFACE FOR THE NEW EDITION

When I started writing this book back in the 1980s, I was concerned with how not only it, but also the very concept of Pagan prayer, would be received. I had often read and heard comments like, "Pagans exercise their own power through magic; they don't grovel before the gods in prayer." This hostility towards prayer disturbed and confused me.

Though I read books on neo-Paganism, I also read books by and about ancient Paganism even more, and one thing I encountered over and over was prayer. All of the Indian Vedas were prayers. Characters in Greek tragedies prayed at the drop of a corpse. Cato provided texts of Roman prayers. And this was just in the Indo-European cultures. Spreading my net wider, I found prayers in the Americas, Africa, the South Pacific, China, Japan—everywhere people held to religions. And not only in the Abrahamic religions, as seem to be believed by many neo-Pagans.

This universality can only be explained, I believe, by an equally universal desire to make contact with the divine, whether seen as personal or not. This desire is found deep within every human being, and comes to the fore in those who are religious.

I needn't have worried. My book fell on fertile ground. Since then, many more Pagans have involved themselves in prayer and in the writing of prayers. While I would like to think that my books played a part in this, I believe that there are other, more powerful factors at work.

First, there is the universal desire to pray. I believe that many Pagans had a hunger that eventually burst forth in the practice of prayer.

Second, I saw the development of a form of Wicca and neo-Paganism that emphasized deities beside the God and the Goddess. This awoke a desire for a personal relationship with them and a need to differentiate between them. It also raised the question of why one would worship different deities; the obvious answer was that they fulfilled different concerns, which led to the need for prayers to address those concerns.

Third, the development of the worship of more than two deities led to more research into the ancient information. This was further inspired by the rise of Reconstructionist Paganism, of people who wanted to worship in ancient ways; their research discovered the importance of praying in Paganism.

Fourth, the mainstreaming of Paganism has decreased the need for Pagans to define themselves by what they *aren't*. This has meant a lessening of wholesale rejection of the practices of other religions.

These factors and no doubt other ones I haven't identified have led to a rebirth of Pagan prayer. Websites, social media, and Pagan magazines now frequently feature prayers, both ancient and modern, and now, given permission to pray, Pagans have responded.

I am obviously happy with this. I believe that it will lead to a deepening not only of our relationships with the sacred beings, but also of our awareness of the sacred in the world we live in. A person who immerses themselves in prayer is immersing themselves in the sacred. This can only be to our benefit.

In writing this and other books, I've learned a lot about prayers. Since this learning hasn't caused me to reject major parts of what is in this book, I haven't made any radical changes to it. I would like to talk a little bit about the changes I *have* made and a little bit about what I've learned about prayer since the book's first publication. In it, I emphasize the function of prayer as communication. Communication has to be between. There is a speaker, and there is a listener or listeners. In prayer, these listeners are the deities, the ancestors, the nature spirits—any or all sacred beings.

But if you look at my prayers, you'll find ones that don't seem to have a sacred audience. These are divided into two types. The first is to things that don't seem to be numinous—a bowl of water, for example. However, anything can be seen as sacred in some way or to some extent. This is like the Shinto idea of a kami; a numinous presence that is possessed by anything special. Not just the sun, not just a mountain like Mt. Fuji, but even a well-made knife or teacup can have (or be, the distinction is not necessary) a kami. This connection may be immediately perceived. But it may be created, especially in the West, by acting as if the kami existed, by talking oneself into belief in its existence. In this way, the entire universe can be made sacred, which is something that many Pagans believe already.

The second exception is one where there seems to be no recipient at all. These prayers come across as simple poems that express a situation. But even here there is a recipient. The situation itself is sacred and may be seen as receiving the prayer. Or the recipients may be all those who hear the prayer, even if it is only a single person. And it is not the ordinary people, but the part of them that is identified as sacred. By treating the person as sacred, they are raised to a status of a numinous being who may appropriately receive prayer.

The most obvious changes that readers of the first edition will notice is that I've rearranged the chapters, rearranged the prayers in the chapters, moved some prayers to different chapters, and created two new chapters from one. I think this makes the book easier to use. The chapters are now arranged similarly to my second book *A Pagan Ritual Prayer Book*; that is, in an order that follows that of a ritual. I moved all the litanies to appropriate chapters, assuming that most people can figure out what prayers can be used. I discovered that some prayers were in the wrong chapters, and fixed that. I realized as I was doing this that the prayers weren't labeled as to the deities they were addressed to and that they weren't in any logical order within each chapter. They are now in the order of General, the God and Goddess, the God, the Goddess, the All-Gods, other deities (alphabetically), the Ancestors, and the Land Spirits. You will also find that I've added a few deities.

I also had the happy opportunity to fix a major problem with the first version. I was appalled to realize after its first publication that there were no prayers for Lugnasad/Lammas and Midsummer. I'd included a prayer for tomato season, but none for two of the eight great neo-Pagan holidays! You'll find prayers for each of these occasions in this edition.

I've only cut one prayer: "The fire of Brighid is the flame on my hearth." It turned out that it was redundant, since it was also the first line of one of the mantras.

If the book interests you, I recommend my second book on prayer, *A Pagan Ritual Prayer Book*. In it you will find more advice on writing prayers and a larger selection of them, with a wider range of deities addressed.

Since the two books were published, I've written many more prayers. I hope some day to be able to publish them, but for now you can find many of them on my Facebook page, where I regularly post them and on my website, *www.ceisiwrserith.com*, through which I can be contacted.

I hope you find this book to be useful on your spiritual journey.

INTRODUCTION

I hope this book is only the first in a long line of books of Pagan prayers, by one author or anthologies, that will come out of our religion as it grows. Prayer is a subject that can never be exhausted. It is a sacred conversation between us and the gods. As long as there have been people, they have conversed with each other and, still, they find things to talk about. Why should we expect sacred conversation to be any different?

I wrote this book with several goals in mind. First, I wanted to explain why prayers and offerings matter, and thereby to encourage others to use them. Second, I wanted to provide the Pagan community with a selection of prayers they could use. And I wanted to show people how they could write their own prayers.

I have tried to be very careful with words in this book. I have sometimes used "gods" instead of "deities" or "gods and goddesses," when the flow of the language seemed to require it. I have even used the politically incorrect phrase "gods and men." For this transgression, I can only ask you to put it beside "deities and people" and see which scans better.

At a number of points, I use the terms "Indo-European" and "Proto-Indo-European." "Indo-European" refers to a family of languages (and cultures) that spreads from India to Europe (thus the name). This family includes Celtic, Norse, Latin, Greek, and Indo-Iranian languages and cultures, as well as others, and, of course, English. "Proto-Indo-European" refers to the language (and culture) from which these are descended. I use these terms because the ancestry, both culturally and genetically, of most of those who read this book will be Indo-European. For that reason, and because this is the group of cultures with which I myself am most comfortable, I will refer to them from time to time, putting things, I hope, into context.

I have added commentaries to some of the prayers to explain the Pagan deities, images, and myths, and to indulge in a little theology. These commentaries also show the connection between myths, images, theology, and prayer, thereby helping you in the construction of your own prayers. I decided to forgo an explanation of neo-Paganism itself, however. There are already enough books out there that do that; I don't have much new to say on the basics. I will say, however, that I believe that Paganism is defined by its rituals rather than its beliefs, so readers will find my thoughts on the subject in the prayers. If you aren't familiar with the basics of neo-Paganism, don't worry; if you read the prayers and my commentaries, you will find the explanations you need.

I've made a slight rearrangement of the order of chapters in this edition. I've put the prayers for the family and the home at the beginning of part II, because it is our home from which we start. I've moved "Litanies and Mantras" to after the chapters on Callings and Praise, because the former can be used for either of the latter.

However, the categories into which I have divided the prayers are not hard and fast. For instance, you can use a prayer of praise as an introduction to one of thanksgiving.

Because of this, you should not feel bound by the chapter titles. Feel free to mix and match, to change and edit, and indeed to make these prayers your own. It is you who will be talking to the gods, and you are the one who will have to answer to them for what you say. Be clear. Be careful in how you pray. Take care how you come before the gods. Give them your best.

PART I

WHY AND HOW WE PRAY

☽ ○ ☾

CHAPTER 1

THE ROLE OF PRAYER—
YESTERDAY AND TODAY

Those of us who call ourselves Pagans owe a debt to all those who came before us. Before trying to define our own, modern Paganism, therefore, we should find out as much as we can about what the ancient Pagans did. To do that, we'll look at their prayers. Then we can either follow their lead, or, if we choose to be different, we can at least choose from knowledge rather than from ignorance.

Ancient Pagan Prayers

The most reliable sources on how the ancient Pagans prayed are the prayers recorded by the Pagans themselves. There are two types of sources of ancient Pagan prayers, the literary and the epigraphic (the ones that were engraved or drawn on things). There are quite a few literary sources for Greek and Roman Paganism, even more for the Egyptian tradition, and a great wealth of material from India. Anthropologists, in modern times, have supplied us with large amounts of material from all over the world. We most certainly do not lack information.

We also have the stories written down in the Middle Ages by monks. These present both problems and benefits, however. When people in Irish stories swear "by the gods my people swear by," are they repeating an ancient Irish oath, or are they simply saying the sort of thing that the monks figured Pagans would say? We don't know. This sort of reference is inspiring, however; if not in substance, at least in style. Maybe these monks were on to something.

The epigraphic evidence comes from inscriptions on offerings, temple walls, etc. Offerings sometimes have a short prayer inscribed on them that gives the name and intent of the offerer. Inscriptions found on temple walls, especially in Egypt, tend to be particularly rich in information.

Even in areas from which information is otherwise scanty, we find examples. We find them in travelers' reports and late versions of myths. Whether we can rely on these sources has long been debated. I personally treat this type of evidence with suspicion, trusting it only when it is supported by other corroborating evidence. Even if this type of evidence does not accurately reflect the culture it claims to depict, however, it can at least tell us how the culture that recorded the stories and reports saw prayer. And this, in turn, can inspire our own prayers.

Two very different sources of information on ancient Pagan prayer are the local styles of modern prayer and surviving folk customs. Many people think that when Christians pray in a particular way in a particular culture, the practice must come from the pre-Christian days of that culture. There is a tendency on the part of writers, especially neo-Pagan writers, to act as if Christians had no creativity of their own. It is very possible, however, that local prayer styles, no matter how ancient they may seem, were invented by Christians rather than Pagans. This doesn't mean we can't use these styles in our own prayers, of course. Never ignore inspiration. Just don't assume you are following some ancient Pagan tradition when you use this sort of source.

Folk customs often contain prayers and songs. But these can present a similar problem. We can rarely know how much of the customs come from a Pagan culture and how much from other sources. To make the situation worse, sometimes the person who recorded the folk material "improved" it, further obscuring its Pagan roots.

So what is a poor Pagan to do? We must educate ourselves as well as we can, using all the sources we can find. We must look carefully at what has been passed on to us from ancient times, weighing its possible antiquity and Pagan nature carefully. Most important of all, however, we must have an active prayer life. We must ask the gods for guidance on how they wish to be prayed to, and we must listen carefully for their answer. Then we must share the results with our fellow Pagans, so that the stock of prayers we hold in common will grow.

Pagan Prayers and Offerings

Almost all religions pray, and most make offerings. Yet a search through the literature of neo-Paganism turns up only a small number of prayers, and even fewer references to offerings. There is much ritual material, to be sure, but the sort in which the worshipper stands before their gods, addresses them with respect, and offers them gifts is in short supply. Invocations, declarations, and spells are found in great number, but acts of praise and devotion, or simply requests rather than demands for help, are not.

This is a modern development, though. A search through the writings of the ancient Pagans turns up huge quantities of prayers. We have inscriptions left by the ancient Celts. We have many prayers from the Greeks; characters in their tragedies were wont to pray at the drop of a corpse. The most ancient Hindu texts, the four Vedas, are essentially long prayer books. From the Americas, from Asia, from Africa, from Oceania, from Australia, we find more and more prayers, building up higher and higher, until we are crushed beneath the obvious: the most common form of Pagan religious expression is prayer.

Closely allied to prayer is the offering—the second most common form of worship. This makes sense; prayers and offerings are the same thing. They both present gifts to the gods—one of words and time, and the other of objects. Prayers usually accompany offerings, and offerings frequently accompany prayers. A line between them cannot be drawn, and I have not tried to do so. When we come before the gods, it is wise not to come empty-handed. We should come bearing, if not objects, then words; if not words, then objects. And how much better if we bring both!

Why Do We Pray?

The ancients may have prayed and made offerings, but what is the point in this modern day and age?

When we pray, we talk to divine beings. They are our spiritual friends or our parents, or our cousins. We talk to our human friends and parents and cousins, so it only makes sense to talk to their divine counterparts as well.

Why do we need to talk in the first place? Don't the gods already know what we want, or how we feel about them? Let's go back to the human equivalent. Do you talk to your friends, or do you just assume they know how you feel and what you want? Do you send notes to your grandparents thanking them for gifts, or do you figure that they'll understand how thankful you are, even if you don't tell them? If Cousin Harry does something great, do you give him a call and say, "Nice going," or do you decide that his own feeling of self-accomplishment should be enough? Surely the gods deserve at least as much consideration as Cousin Harry!

Maybe the problem is the way you see the divine beings. Our gods are not omniscient. Unlike Santa Claus, they don't see you when you're sleeping, or know when you're awake. They have to be invited into your life. Go on, give them a call and tell them how much you've missed them; tell them how wonderful you think they are; and, while you're at it, maybe ask for a favor or thank them for favors done. You might find you like talking to them.

Why Do We Make Offerings?

While the "why" of prayer may be pretty obvious, the "why" of offerings is a bit harder to see. Why would the gods need, or even want, our gifts? What can a spiritual being do with a bottle of wine or a piece of art?

The various Pagan religions give a variety of reasons for making offerings. Each justifies the practice according to its own theology and social structure. Neo-Pagans, with their lack of common theology and without a distinct society, have to review the many reasons given by other traditions to decide which ones are acceptable. When we do this, we may find our beliefs regarding the gods changing. A god we make offerings to is different from a god we don't. Since Paganism is a religion of action rather than belief, this is to be expected. What matters is that we do the right thing.

Why do the gods demand material gifts from us, then? Why are they not satisfied with prayer and a sincere heart? In part it's because there is no sharp line to be drawn between the material and the spiritual. By demanding material offerings, the gods remind us that the material is sacred too.

Offering material gifts also ensures sincerity. Anyone can give words, and anyone can pretend sincerity, but to give something valuable that we own shows we care for the gods at least as much as for our material possessions.

When we make offerings, we take part in the way of nature. For, just as there is a mystery in the natural order of eating and being eaten, so too there is a mystery in the natural dynamic of giving and receiving gifts—not in the sense of "you wash my hands and I'll wash yours," but rather, the same hands that reach out to give also reach out to receive.

We must enter into this reciprocal relationship with the gods in order for them to become active in our lives. They long for this, waiting for us to approach them with gift-laden arms. This is, quite likely, the origin of the sacred nature of hospitality. The gods are the ultimate hosts, inviting us in when we knock. We must be the best of guests, returning their generosity by acting as hosts in turn. It is the bonds of hospitality that tie people together and communicate the truth that they are not so separate after all. Or, it may have been the other way round. Hospitality may have been sacred before the practice of offerings. If so, then the giving of offerings is simply a case of hospitality toward the gods. We invite them into our lives and, as their hosts, we give them gifts.

The "Politics" of Giving

An offering is frequently used to establish a relationship between a worshipper and the gods of a place. Take, for example, the Roman custom of sacrificing to Silvanus, the god of forests, before clearing land. He had to be satisfied, and even invited to stay on the land once the woods were gone.

An offering is an act of completion. So many things come to us from the gods. If we keep them, the flow ends there. By holding tightly to the gifts of the gods, we create an interruption in the natural rhythm of the world, a dead-end into which the universe flows and then stops.

Neo-Pagans, though, are dedicated to the idea of circles and cycles, of things changing and transforming. They believe there are no dead-ends in nature. Even if we hold tightly to our possessions, of course, in the end, we will be cheated. We will die, and they will go to others. The gods will not allow a dead-end to persist; they will not permit interruptions of their cycles.

This is not something we can take comfort in, as we grasp our goods ever more tightly. If we are indeed Pagans, then we must live the way the gods want us to live. While we are alive, we must not be "dead-ends." We must give freely of what we have, to each other and to the gods. When we make offerings, we tell the gods that we know this, and we remind ourselves of it, so we will be less likely to do the wrong thing in the future. Such a wonderful return from so small a gift as a glass of milk, a bowl of grain, a painted stone!

What you give as an offering must be of some value to you and of presumed value to the being you offer it to. I am well aware that there are cultures in which it is considered perfectly appropriate to give symbolic offerings—paper money, for instance. I have always had trouble understanding the logic behind this. Some explain it in this way. The act of offering itself is a gift, intended to arouse an obligation of a return gift. In gift exchanges, it is considered proper for a giver who is higher in station to give the most valuable gift—a form of noblesse oblige. For the giver of the lower order to give too generously would be ostentatious, especially if the gift is more valuable than that of the higher being. Since humans are considered to be, by definition, on a much lower level than the gods, the proper offerings for them are insignificant ones.

Some individuals, and indeed entire cultures, have reasoned like this, to the point of saying that the gods are so much greater than us that any real gift we give is too much. This strikes me, however, as too clever by half. A gift with no value is no gift at all. There is no circumstance in which such a gift is appropriate, unless a return gift of no value is desired.

Another explanation is that the gods need only spiritual goods, so they are content with symbolic offerings. This explanation is dangerous. It insults the material realm, making it appear insignificant in relation to the spiritual. It makes offerings meaningless; if the gods desire only symbols, why bother? Why not just pray to them? And if the gift is only a symbol, what does a worthless gift symbolize?

Give to the gods, then, and not of worthless things. Give your best, and know that what the gods give you will always be greater than anything you can give them. You won't insult them by giving them too much.

Do the Pagan Gods Exist?

How we answer this question will determine the types of rituals we perform. In answering the questions "Why do we pray?" and "Why do we make offerings?" I assumed a belief in the gods to which we pray and give gifts. What is not always appreciated is that the reverse is often true. The very acts of praying and offering can arouse beliefs in us. When we pray and make offerings, the response both from the gods and from ourselves may well answer the question of just who and what the gods are. Perhaps out of the writing and use of prayers, a new form of neo-Pagan piety will arise.

Writing neo-Pagan prayers presents special difficulties. The prayers of many religions incorporate mythical themes, either making reference to myths or actually telling them. Although neo-Paganism has embraced many ancient myths, Wicca, the most widespread form of neo-Paganism, has few myths of its own. I have dealt with this in several ways.

First, not all prayers incorporate myths. Nor is it true that all rituals are enactments of myths. Second, there are indeed some Wiccan myths—the most obvious being the Legend of the Descent of the Goddess and the myth of the year implied in Wiccan rituals. Third, there are the myths told about ancient deities. Although not actually absorbed into Wicca, these deities find devotees among neo-Pagans, who might therefore be expected to be interested in prayers to their favorite deities.

In this book, I have also taken elements that are found in a number of myths and applied them to the Wiccan God and Goddess. Essentially, what I am doing here is writing new myths for Wicca. I think it best to be honest about this. Although Wiccans may draw inspiration from many myths, Wicca, as such, is myth-impoverished. A minor goal of this book is to show how that can be corrected.

Of course, the divine beings to whom these prayers are addressed are not just the Wiccan God and Goddess. Worshippers from many of the modern Pagan religions will find prayers to their deities here. I hope that those who encounter deities from traditions other than their own will be inspired to pull out some mythology books and learn more. Learning is never a waste of time.

To Whom Do We Pray?

One way to divide the types of beings Pagans pray to, the numina, is to split them into three categories: the High Gods, the Ancestors, and the spirits.

The High Gods fall into two categories: the God and Goddess of Wicca (the archetypal male and female) and the gods of the ancient Pagan pantheons—Brighid, Mithra, Isis, and so on. I obviously couldn't write prayers to all of the ancient deities, so instead I wrote prayers in part to those who appealed to me personally, but also to those who are popular among other Pagans, even if they aren't part of my own pantheon. There is a short glossary of the deities in appendix II. Maybe one you've never heard of before will strike your fancy.

The Ancestors may either be those of a particular family or those of us all—a genetic ancestor or a cultural one. For instance, George Washington has no genetic descendants, but he is a cultural ancestor of all Americans. When I use the term "Ancestors," I usually mean genetic ancestors, but there are always cultural implications as well. After all, we are, in the end, one family.

The spirits are a miscellaneous category identified primarily by their limits. Instead of being the gods of a people, they are peculiar to a locale or an object. They may be associated with a tool or a weapon, or they may be connected with a place. You may wish to pray to the spirit who inhabits an impressive tree near your house, or those who live in the woods you visit on a camping trip.

Let me illustrate the differences between the High Gods and the spirits with an example. One of the early Norse settlers in Iceland was a worshipper of Thor. When he emigrated, he took with him the pillar from his temple. As he approached the coast, he threw the pillar overboard and allowed it to float to the shore. In this way, Thor himself chose the settler's landing spot. As a High God, Thor came to the new land with his worshippers.

The Land Spirits, on the other hand, had been left behind to dwell in the places with which they were associated. In the new land, the Norse discovered new holy places and established relationships with the spirits of these new shrines. They had left behind the spirits who lived in the burial mounds, stones, and forests of their old home, so they sought out those who lived in their new one.

These are the different kinds of beings Pagans pray to. They are all worthy of prayers and offerings. I guarantee that, if you give them a chance, if you talk to them and give them gifts, your life will be greatly enriched.

☽ ○ ☾

CHAPTER 2

THE BASICS
OF PRAYER

In chapter 1, I talked about why we pray. Now it's time to talk about how we pray.

Praying through Words

If prayer is communication with a divine being, and if we usually communicate in words, our prayers will consist primarily of words. There are many ways to speak words in a prayer. You can speak them loudly, proclaiming to everyone (even if you are alone) what you have to say. You can speak them softly, indicating a desire for intimacy with the divine being to whom you pray. You can pray in a sing-song voice, perhaps accompanied by a rocking motion. This adds a rhythm to your words that may express the rhythms of nature you are trying to express. You may even pray silently, in your mind. In public, this may be your only option. In private, however, it may express a desire for an intimacy even greater than that which you get from speaking softly. It may even be that the state in which you find yourself makes your voice seem shocking and disturbing.

Whatever voice you use to pray, I recommend speaking distinctly. Worshippers in some traditions tend to mumble their prayers; some of the prayers in Zoroastrian rituals are deliberately said in that way. If you pray the same prayer over and over on one occasion, you may eventually start to slur your words. That is fine; what happens is that you begin to go beyond words. You should start out in a clear voice, however, making sure that you and the one to whom you pray know exactly what is being said.

It isn't necessary to pay attention to each word. Sometimes too much attention can get in the way of feeling; you focus on the mental side of things, letting the emotional and spiritual elements fall away. Sometimes, however, a word jumps out of your prayer to shock you, making you realize something about it that you'd never realized before. This is one of the truly wonderful possibilities of prayer. This kind of insight can help you to understand just what it is you are saying to the being you are praying to. In fact, this insight may very well be a gift from that being, a gift of understanding that will affect your prayer life from that moment on. Don't just listen to the words you are saying then; listen for any answer to them.

As with all conversation, though, prayer can involve much more than words. Making an offering, for instance, can be thought of as praying with an object. The gods may be prayed to with dance, or with music, or with gestures. Even when words are involved, any of these other methods of prayer may be used as well.

In fact, it is virtually impossible to pray with words alone. After all, your body must be in some position when the words are spoken or thought. This position is an integral part of your prayer. This is especially true for Pagans—the gods reveal themselves to us in bodies, and it is with our bodies that we pray to them. By this, I mean both that we come before the gods in bodies, and that we also use our bodies to pray to them. The position you use "prays" as much as the words you say.

Praying through Posture

Think of it in everyday terms. When you are called into your boss's office, do you slouch or stand respectfully? When you are at a presentation, what message do you convey when you lounge in your chair? How different is the message if you lean forward and fix your eyes on the presenter? Since you communicate in many ways, it is a good idea to make sure that all the messages you send say the same thing.

In Western culture, the body position most identified with praying is kneeling. Many Pagans hesitate to adopt this posture because it seems to subordinate us, to make us slaves to the gods. There are, however, many ways in which the gods are indeed superior to us (why would we want to worship beings who weren't?). To acknowledge that superiority is, therefore, appropriate. I, myself, do not kneel, but for another reason entirely: I identify the position too strongly with the religion of my youth, and the theological implications are too great for me to overcome. Still, I find a semi-kneeling position, in which

I sit on my heels, to be a very good way to pray; it is both relaxed and attentive. It show the gods that I will pay attention to them, and that I am willing to wait a long time if need be. Perhaps as more children are raised as Pagans, they will not resist kneeling, and the position will make its way back into our prayers.

A position that may seem even more demeaning, but that is still appropriate for Pagan prayer, is prostration. To some, lying flat on the floor, face down, may seem a little like groveling. There are times, however, when the presence of the deity so overpowers you that there is no response more appropriate than prostration. At such moments, you only want to sink into their presence, and prostration is the way your body does this. It lets you acknowledge the deity's presence with your entire self: mind, spirit, and body. The somewhat old-fashioned word "swoon" comes to mind.

One famous prayer posture is the lotus position, in which you intertwine your legs like a pretzel (literally), prop yourself up so that both knees touch the floor, straighten your spine, lower your chin a little, and put your hands in your lap. Although this is a position traditionally more common for meditation than for prayer (I don't want to get into the differences and similarities between the two here), it also makes a great posture for praying. It is stable, and with much practice can even become comfortable. Moreover, it is conducive to waiting; in fact, it conveys nothing better than expectant but patient waiting. It says, "Come when you will, and you will find me here." It allows you to express respect without abasing yourself.

A prayer posture that was very common in ancient times is standing with your upper arms parallel to the ground, your elbows bent upward, and your hands open with palms forward. This posture is so identified with prayer that it is called the *orans*, or "praying" position. Standing in this position, you are again expectant, on your feet and waiting for the deity to come. You are ready to do the spirit's bidding, approaching as a subordinate without abasing yourself. You both give respect and expect to receive it. You hold up your hands in respectful greeting. You are clearly unarmed; you do not presume to threaten the deity (as if you could). You stand ready to give or to receive. This position is acceptable for most deities; some, such as many of the Indo-European gods, consider it the best position for prayer.

Whether you pray to a High God, an Ancestor, or a spirit can determine which position is best. Attitudes of prostration are appropriate only for the High Gods. When calling an Ancestor, a position of respectful waiting is good. It is like waiting for a beloved grandparent—you have the right, by long association and familiarity, to take almost any attitude, but you choose to take a respectful one—not out of fear or awe, but out of love and honor. You do it because it is right to do so. As you work with Ancestors, you may find yourself on more familiar terms with them, and relax with them. Still, it never hurts to be polite. Remember, these beings were once like us. You know how you would be like to be treated; show them at least as much respect.

The spirits are an odd case. Their influence is limited to an area, an object, an event, but within that context, they are very powerful. When in their area of action, therefore, treat them as if they were deities. They are, in fact, just that within their respective realms.

Positions can be varied within a prayer. You may call the deity standing in the *orans* position, drop to a lotus position, and then prostrate yourself. You send out the call in a posture of respectful address, await the response in a posture of attentive waiting, and take an attitude of amazement at the wonder of the deity's presence. Note how, at each step, you are communicating with your body. You come before the deity united in mind, body, and soul: as an integrated human being. All of your being is directed toward communication with the deity.

Praying through Motion

Motion can be a prayer in itself, even without words. The gods understand the language of motion just as well as that of words. Moreover, words and motion can express the same thought. It is common practice in rituals to have this sort of redundancy, in which one meaning is embedded in more than one symbol. The meaning is thus strengthened, and all of you becomes involved in the prayer. A prayer that is only in the mind is a prayer that is not truly alive.

I have already shown how more than one posture can be appropriate during a prayer. Consider, then, the possibility that moving from one position to another may have meaning—that the actual motion itself can convey a message. At the most basic level, the fact that you make a change from one posture to another indicates that the change matters enough to justify making extra effort. It shows that you care enough to know which posture is appropriate for which portion of your prayer.

More subtle is the effect that the motion itself can have. You may start out in a sitting position, then rise. With the rising of your body comes a rising of your spirit, which goes to the gods and enters into their presence. You sit, and this causes a drawing into yourself, through which the gods are invited in. Motions can thus have not so much a meaning as an effect.

One common motion is circumambulation. This is a delightful word that means "walking around something." To circumambulate is to honor that which is circumambulated—an image, a sacred spot, a fire. Walking around a place is a very common way of honoring the spirit associated with the place.

The proper direction to walk, in the Indo-European traditions at least, is clockwise. (If you work within a different tradition, study it closely enough to be certain whether the direction matters.) There are, I think, two reasons for this. First, the Sun travels clockwise in the northern hemisphere. Thus, to move about something in this direction is to invoke the power of nature. You become the Sun, and the object or place circumambulated becomes that which the Sun orbits. Second—and I think that this is more important—moving around something clockwise means that your right side is always toward it. With apologies to the left-handed, in many traditions the right is the favored side. To put one's right side toward something is to honor it; to put one's left side toward it is to dishonor it.

There are times when it is appropriate to circumambulate counterclockwise, however. This is not only dishonoring, it is disestablishing. Counterclockwise motion breaks things up and opens them. It can thus be used to open a doorway into the other realm through which prayers may pass. One warning, though: once this doorway is open and something comes through, you must reverse direction and honor the deity or spirit thus summoned.

Praying through Dance

The ultimate form of praying with motion is dance. Dance has traditionally been used in many ways in many cultures. Each position of the dance may be intended to communicate something, the individual motions working together to make up a complete message, in much the same way that words combine to make a sentence. Or the message may, as in the more stationary kind of motion I mentioned above, be expressed by the dance as a whole.

Dance, when used in prayer, is most often meant to express emotion. Any emotion can be expressed through movement—from joy, to grief, to awe. The emotion you feel will usually tell you the right way to move if you listen to it.

Dance can also express an attribute of the deity invoked, or be a way of calling in itself. For instance, deities of war are, oddly enough, often associated with dance—dance of a martial character, to be sure, but dance nonetheless. In Rome, in March and October, priests of Mars, the Salii, went about Rome performing a dance (in a 3/4, i.e., waltz, rhythm), in full armor no less. This dance honored Mars, and served to invoke his blessing on Rome as well.

Dance can also serve as an offering. It involves an expenditure of time and energy, and is a form of art. Any honor or recognition you may receive from others when you pray (if this is a public prayer) is dedicated to the deity to whom you pray. When you dance to the point of exhaustion, the dance not only serves as an offering, but can also open you up to the deity. Through the dance, you give all of yourself, creating a space for the deity to fill.

Praying through Music

Dance generally requires music of some sort. In many traditions, in fact, prayers are sung or chanted. Vedic mantras, for instance, are always sung. American Indian prayers are often chanted. And some of the greatest music of the Western world is no more than musical prayer—Mozart's Requiem, for example. Different cultures and traditions have given different reasons for why music can enhance or empower prayer. In some Greek mystery religions, certain notes were thought to correspond to different aspects of the universe, or even to an Ultimate Reality. But there are practical reasons for the linkages between music and prayer as well. It is easier, for instance, to remember a song than a paragraph. Moreover, music cuts deeper than simple words. It has a power to move that is entirely separate from the words set to it. How much better, then, if the words and music convey the same message?

Most of us, however, are not Mozart and aren't apt to produce a Requiem. (Budding Mozarts out there, please get to work and write us a few good sung prayers.) In the meantime, what is a poor Pagan to do?

If you worship in a tradition that has its own style of music, you already have the answer. For those of us who are following a European path, I recommend Gregorian chant. Yes, this is traditionally a Christian form of music, but it may have Pagan roots. I have heard Sanskrit chanting and very old Irish a cappella music. They both sound remarkably like Gregorian chant. I have it on pretty good authority that both reconstructed Old English music and ancient Greek music do too. I'm no musicologist, but if this is true, then Gregorian chant draws on an ancient European musical tradition. As such, it can serve as a powerful tool for Pagan prayer. Go ahead and use it. There are plenty of recordings; get some and listen until you have a feel for it.

Praying through Gestures

Somewhere between postures and motions fall gestures. Things done with the hands and arms have their own meaning. These gestures can be passive or active. For instance, there is the classic Christian posture of folded hands. This communicates a pleading attitude, but it can also convey a certain defenselessness, so it may not be a gesture you want to use.

The *orans* position described earlier is a good replacement for the folded hands gesture. In this position you come before the gods unarmed and open, but not in abasement. You do not plead; you approach with respect, and ask for a certain amount of respect yourself.

The very fact that your hands are still, whether in the *orans* position or resting in your lap if you are sitting, conveys a message. You are not attempting to do something, but rather are waiting for the deities to perform some act. You have stilled your hands, and now you wait.

Moving hands, however, are sometimes more appropriate in other situations. They can constitute a little dance—a dance performed with only one part of your body, to be sure, but a dance nonetheless. For instance, you can start with your hands clasped together chest-high—you begin your prayer at rest. Then throw your arms wide—send your words out. Then bring them back into the *orans* position—you wait, ready to greet the spirit you called when it arrives.

Giving offerings always involves hand movements. You may place something in or on the earth; you may pour it out; you may throw it into a fire or body of water. Think about what each of these gestures means to you, and you will understand your offering better.

When you make an offering, you pray with objects. When you assume a posture, you pray with your body. When you speak, you pray with your mind. When you pray with objects, your body, and your mind, you pray with your soul. Your soul rises up into the presence of the gods and communes with them; you speak, or just rest in their presence. It's a beautiful thing.

☽ ○ ☾

CHAPTER 3

PREPARING
FOR PRAYER

When you pray, you come before the gods. You enter into their presence so that you can give them a message or offering. It is common to perform some act or preliminary ritual to prepare yourself for the encounter.

In many religions, this is done by washing or donning special clothes. Frequently, this is prompted by a belief that dirt or ordinary clothing can pollute and must, therefore, be removed before the sacred can be contacted—either because the pollution will prevent the contact, or because the deities, once contacted, will be offended. Many neo-Pagans, however, believe that the material realm is as sacred as the spiritual, and that the deities are not offended by it. In fact, many believe that the deities are intimately involved in the material realm, forming its very substance.

These preparatory steps are often taken as much for the sake of the worshippers as for the worshipped. The cares of everyday life can intrude on your relationship with the sacred. A ritual act such as washing or putting on clean clothes can help you to free your thoughts from everyday obsessions and set them toward the gods. Ritual words of preparation can help you concentrate your mind in the right direction, so that the intent of your prayer is clear, both to you and to the gods. The gods know this, and might quite justifiably be insulted if you can't be bothered to take the time to get ready for prayer.

The ancient Pagans certainly understood the value of preparation. For instance, in Iceland, it was forbidden to look on the holy spot of assembly unwashed. In Rome, priests placed a fold of their clothing over their heads before prayers. (This was primarily to prevent ill omens from being heard or seen during the prayer, but such a practical act had a psychological and spiritual effect as well; it cut the worshipper off from everyday distractions.) In Greece, a ribbon was frequently put around the forehead before sacrifices.

Purification

The most common form of preparation is purification. This is done most easily by washing. Some Indian tribes purified with smoke, often from burning sage. This form of purification is also used in Catholic high Masses, where a censer is taken around the altar and swung toward the congregation.

Pagans who work with the four elements of air, fire, water, and earth can use both methods, one after the other. When you dissolve salt in water, it becomes a mixture of earth and water; when you burn incense, you combine fire and air. To use these mixtures to purify yourself, anoint your body (traditionally your forehead, lips, and heart) with the salt water while saying:

> *With the power of the sea,*
> *that washes the shores,*
> *I am purified.*

Then move the incense so its smoke passes over your body, while saying:

> *May I be pure,*
> *may all my impurities be burned away,*
> *carried away on the incense smoke.*

In many traditions, however, water alone is considered sufficient. Roman and Greek temples often had bowls of water placed outside them for this purpose, as Catholic churches often do today. They also had signs, some of which have survived, that listed other requirements. In one case, for instance, those who had had sexual intercourse within the last twenty-four hours were forbidden to enter. The moral here is not that sex is necessarily impure, but that, if these signs were necessary, we can be sure that different deities had different requirements for prayer. Some deities might, by their very nature, be repelled by some things. A deity of lust might be repelled by someone who is celibate, for instance.

The best advice is to research the deities you want to pray to, and find out what form of purification they prefer.

If there is no way to find this out, you can fall back on using water. You can wash your hands or anoint yourself while saying something like:

> *May I be pure,*
> *fit to approach the gods.*

A variation on the Greek practice of donning a ribbon is to wear special garments or jewelry. These can be as elaborate as the robes used by ceremonial magicians, or as simple as the traditional Greek headband. With repeated use, these items become a signal that prayer time has arrived. Whatever accessories are used, their donning should be accompanied with a ritual utterance. A simple example for donning a headband might be:

> *I am encircled with the sacred,*
> *girded about, encompassed,*
> *that my actions here today*
> *might be within the sacred way.*

An example for putting on ceremonial robes might be:

> *The sacred covers me,*
> *I am surrounded by the pure.*

Ceremonial jewelry can include images of deities, items associated with deities (a Thor's hammer, for instance), and general symbols of life, power, or spirituality (such as a pentagram or a triskele). I wear an image of Cernunnos. A devotee of the Egyptian Ma'at might wear a silver feather, to represent her feather of truth. You can wear this jewelry only for prayers, to put yourself in an instant prayer mode, or you can wear it all the time, making your whole life a time of prayer. Either way, it is a good idea to don these items in a prayerful manner. For instance, when I put on my Cernunnos image each morning, I say:

> *My lord Cernunnos, I offer you my worship.*
> *Watch over me today as I go about my affairs:*
> *keep me safe, keep me happy, keep me healthy.*

Someone putting on a Ma'at feather might pray:

> *Lady of Truth, be with me today.*
> *As I wear your feather, guard my words and deeds.*
> *May what I say and what I do*
> *be in accord with your sacred law.*

You might use these words while putting on a pentagram:

> *The elements are joined with the power of spirit.*
> *May I be blessed by the four.*
> *May I be blessed by spirit.*
> *May I be blessed by the five.*

Purification and the use of sacred jewelry or dress are not mutually exclusive. They both encourage detaching from the distractions of everyday life and coming into the presence of the divine. Indo-European cultures, though, make a distinction between the sacred and the holy. They define the sacred as the dangerous power of the divine, which must be dealt with first. Only then can the holy, the blessing power of the divine, be acquired. Purification enables us to cross over into the sacred. Putting on special jewelry or clothing puts you in touch with the holy. If you do both, you acknowledge both aspects of the divine.

Creating a Sacred Space

A third type of preparation for prayer is the creation of sacred space. A sacred space is one cut off from normal space in some way. You can create this by putting yourself in the center of the universe and then organizing it around you in the way envisioned by your tradition. This has nothing to do with the actual physical layout of the universe, but instead expresses a tradition's symbolic system. For instance, Wiccans associate the four directions with elements, colors, spirits, tools, etc. A preparatory prayer for a Wiccan might involve becoming aware of these symbols and putting them, either mentally or physically, in their proper places.

Putting yourself at the center of the universe has a number of effects. First, it tells you who and where you are. Any relationship, including those with the divine, must start from that place. By expressing this awareness in a prayer, you establish it ritually, and you can then slide right into the rest of your prayers. Another advantage of centering yourself in this way is that it can be very calming. It can remove distractions, allowing you to concentrate on what you are about to do.

Finally, the sacred center is the place at which the divine power enters the universe. It is the hub about which all the rest turns. It is where the gods can be approached. By locating yourself there, you increase your chances of being able to commune with them. Perhaps they can talk to you wherever you are, but can you talk to them?

This is a centering prayer that can be used by a number of traditions, including Wicca:

> *I place myself in the center of the world,*
> *where pillar and cauldron are joined, overflowing,*
> *continually pouring over, and sending waves of*
> *   existence out into the world.*
> *Before I perform my acts of worship, I take you into*
> *   myself,*
> *that what I do might be equally productive*
> *and out of me might flow wonders.*

This prayer includes a description of a mythical conception of the universe. Here, existence is born of the joining of a pillar and a cauldron. In Wicca, these represent the God (pillar) and Goddess (cauldron). These images are found in other traditions, so this prayer may be appropriate for them as well. For instance, the pillar might be the Norse World Tree, the cauldron the well of Mimir at its base. Similarly, the pillar might be the tent pole up which a shaman flies on his spirit journey. The cauldron might be the cup or bowl from which inspiring drink is consumed, that from which sacred mead or soma is drunk. Here is another prayer, appropriate for both Wicca and shamanic traditions:

> *To the east, to the south,*
> *to the west, to the north,*
> *to above and below,*
> *I send my words flying.*
> *From the east, from the south,*
> *from the west, from the north,*
> *from above and below,*
> *may blessings come flying.*

Reconstructionists of the Celtic or other Indo-European traditions might use:

> *The waters support and surround me.*
> *The land extends about me.*
> *The sky reaches out above me.*
> *At the center burns a living flame.*

Centering prayers can also be used to place the universe in relation to a social structure. For instance:

> *World below, watery world, with chaos and order*
> *   overflowing,*
> *bring true creation into my life, with order and*
> *   beauty,*
> *with power and grace.*
> *World above, far-flung heavens, ordering the world*

with might and law,
bring true stability into my life, with law and structure,
with clarity and reason.
World about me, far-extending, with land well-set,
bring true being into my life, with help and love,
with health and prosperity.

It is a little presumptuous, of course, to create your own sacred space at a place that is already holy in some way. Catholics, for instance, wouldn't re-consecrate an altar in a cathedral each time they went in to pray. Since Pagans revere many natural holy sites, this is an important point for them to remember. You may find yourself in front of a magnificent tree or at the edge of a deep lake, recognize that it is holy, and want to pray. It would be a bit rude to ask that the site conform to your own way of organizing sacred space. The right thing would be to conform yourself to the place, rather than trying to make the place conform to your needs.

To honor such a space, first quiet yourself. Sit comfortably and quietly. Keep your body still. Then listen—not only with your ears, but with your whole body and your soul. A wind blowing over a stone may sound like something speaking to you. The sun striking a tree may raise a scent from the bark. The light on moving water may form a pattern. You may not understand the language in which the message is expressed, but something will indeed speak to you. Listen to it and appreciate the beauty of the expression, even if you don't know its meaning.

After you have listened, it is time for you to give back. You can start with a short prayer of praise, or one of calling. You'll find examples in later chapters. You can say something as simple as:

> *You who live in the depths of this lake,*
> *I sit and think of you*
> *and honor you as you deserve to be honored.*

It is always good to follow this prayer with an offering. You are offering to the local spirits, so your offering should be appropriate to the place. In the United States, corn (maize) is right, as is tobacco. In Europe, try wheat or oats. Bread is good anywhere, and coins also seem to be universally appreciated.

If you decide to mark out an outside space for ritual, either as a permanent place of worship or for a specific ritual more complex than a single prayer, you should make offerings to the Land Spirits. Otherwise, you are essentially stealing the land. To use the space for worshipping the gods without making offerings to the Land Spirits would be a little like going over the head of your boss to speak to the president of the company. Your boss wouldn't like it; the president wouldn't like it; and, in the end, you wouldn't like it. Always make offerings to the local spirits. It's the polite thing to do.

Sacred Flame

Fire plays a very important role in many religions, and Paganism is no exception. Light, in general, is associated with the gods, and the presence of light with the presence of the gods. Fire is warmth, and warmth is life. In the presence of the gods, we feel alive. Fire is also a means of giving offerings. Our words go through the flames to the gods; through the fire, they are transformed into spiritual offerings. Sometimes, the offering is to the fire itself, either as an element or as deity. Thus, an offering in fire feeds the fire, the deities to whom it is offered through the fire, or both.

The lighting of a sacred flame often plays a part in the creation of a sacred space. The flame may rise from a candle, or an oil lamp, or, if possible, an actual fire, either on a hearth or as an outdoor campfire.

Obviously, any offering given through fire must be flammable. Sometimes such offerings are fuels, such as vegetable or olive oil, or clarified butter. (Please do not pour something as flammable as lighter fluid, distilled spirits, alcohol, or petroleum products on a fire. The gods aren't anxious to have you as a burnt offering.) Non-dairy creamer, surprisingly, makes an excellent offering, feeding the fire very nicely. Incense, paintings, grains, and prayers written on paper or wood also make excellent offerings.

Here are some prayers to go with fire offerings:

> *I feed you with oil, fire of oblation,*
> *that you might grow strong,*
> *that you might grow bright,*
> *that you might carry my prayers to the gods.*

$$\mathrm{\,D\,O\,C}$$

> *Take this, fire;*
> *eat it and do not forget my generosity,*
> *but carry my wishes to the gods*
> *and say to them that I am your friend,*

a giver of gifts,
who deserves their kind consideration.

☽ ○ ☾

Speak with your many tongues,[1]
carrying my prayers to the gods.
Take your share of my offering,
conveying the rest faithfully
to those to whom I offer it.
Fire of offering,
perform these deeds truly
as you have always done.

Using Preparatory Prayers

Prayers of sacred space may be said between purification and the rest of your prayers, to establish yourself in the universe before calling on the gods. Or they may be said after the gods are called, since it is the power of the gods that allows the universe to be ordered. If you do not wish to create sacred space, you can use openings such as these:

Surrounded by all the numinous beings of earth and
*   sky and water,*
I pray with confidence, for I know their help is
*   certain.*

☽ ○ ☾

I place myself at your service,
gods of my people.
Open me to your wishes,
make me a conduit for your will,
bringing forth your desires in the human world.

The following prayers can be used with an offering:

This goes before me, opening the door.
Key to the gods, be my way-shower.

☽ ○ ☾

Hidden in the folds of the land you dwell
and have dwelt since the world began.
I am one of the world's younger children
come to honor you with these offerings.

☽ ○ ☾

Whether god or goddess who rules this place,
to you I offer my friendship
and with it this gift.

☽ ○ ☾

Gateway of the gods, receive my offering.
As it sinks deep with you, let it open the door,
and let it be carried to them whom I praise in
*   this way.*

Large bodies of water are traditional places for offering. Offerings in rivers or the ocean may be given as prayers or as thanks for successful crossings, or they may be given to the spirit of the river as an apology for building a bridge.

Purification, the creation of sacred space, lighting a fire, and introductory prayers are all good ways to prepare for major prayers. They make the prayers themselves into little rituals, placing them in the context of your entire religious system. They are a very good way to begin scheduled rituals, such as morning or evening prayers.

I can hear you saying, "But what if I just need to pray at a moment's notice?" Don't worry. These preparations are not absolutely necessary. There will be times when you simply won't have the time or the means to prepare for prayer. As an extreme example, when your car is sliding into another on an icy road, there isn't exactly time to do a purification ritual. "Isis, help" may be all you can get out. And since that is perfectly in tune with what is happening, it is a perfect prayer.

If you have the time and the means, though, something more becomes appropriate. Part of living a Pagan life is doing that which is just right for the moment. Doing a more complete ritual when you can is just right for *that* moment.

The gods appreciate effort. They like to see that we are willing to take the time to do everything possible. You may find that your prayers yield more blessings if you perform the preparatory rituals whenever you can—not because the gods can't give you what you want without them, but because there is little motivation for them to do so if you can't even make the effort to prepare yourself to contact them. And don't you want to make an effort? Aren't they worth it?

Even if your prayer isn't a request for anything, you will be given benefits—an increased sense of knowing your place in the universe, a stronger awareness of the presence of the gods, a development of your spiritual discipline. When praying, try to make a full-fledged ritual out of your prayer whenever possible. The benefits are real, and well worth the trouble.

CHAPTER 4

COMPOSING PRAYERS

At their simplest, prayers are just talking to the gods. You think about them and you talk. But the gods are different from us. Talking to them is, therefore, different from talking to people. You can show this by using a different style of speech when addressing them. Just as you have set aside time and space for this sacred conversation, you set aside your normal way of speech to make your prayers special.

Because prayer is communication with a divine being, and because Pagans are polytheistic, Pagan prayers must identify the being to whom they are addressed. Whether the gods need this or not is not the question. If you reach out to deities, it is only polite to call them by name. No sense starting out on the wrong foot.

Identifying Your Gods

The gods you recognize help to define the universe as you see it. Do you recognize a deity of government? The name of this deity can tell you a lot about what you think of government. Most people don't know that the Roman god Mars was not just a god of war, but was also connected with agriculture. The Romans saw a connection there, and by calling on Mars, they recognized that connection. Even if the gods don't need to be identified exactly, it is a good thing for you to do so.

Gods don't have to be identified by name; they can frequently be identified by title or function. The hearth goddess Brighid may be addressed, for instance, as "Lady of Fire." Dionysos may be called "You who watch over our vines, who flow with the sap." Isis might be called "You in whose wings we find safety." Just as good thank you notes do not have to start with the words "thank you," so a prayer does not have to start with the name of the deity. You might start with something like "I who stand before you, I who come into your presence, I who am your worshipper, call out to you, Mithra." The name should come relatively early in the prayer, however. No sense building up too much suspense.

In most cases, though, it is best to start with the deity's name or a title. This is good both for you and for the deity. For you, it serves to focus your intent. For the deity, it serves to bring you to his or her attention. There is no sense making all the deities listen to all our prayers on the off chance that they might be involved. They are not unlimited, even if they are vastly greater than we are.

Deities are frequently named more than once in a prayer, although not usually by the same name. Repeating the same name can make the prayer tedious and one-dimensional. Moreover, you risk getting only a partial understanding of a deity if you use only one means of identification. Divine beings are far more complicated than that. It is more effective to give your deities titles that describe their attributes or relate myths associated with them. For instance, Apollo might be addressed in this way: "Sweet-songed Apollo, heal me. I come before you, Lord of the Bow, whose arrows bring healing. I ask that you help me, Leto's son: heal my own child."

Some ancient prayers are essentially long lists of such titles. Such lists are very useful for calling or praising a deity. They can become boring, but boredom can be a good thing; it can turn off your mind and release your spirit. Besides, when a prayer works, and the presence of the deity becomes obvious, it quickly stops being boring. The piling up of title after title can build to a level of ecstasy, as the person praying becomes more and more aware of the deity's power and presence. A tension is created as each title reveals a new piece of the deity's identity, until the tension is released and the prayer goes on its way, an arrow loosed from the bow of your words.

Defining Deities through Their Myths

The defining of a deity may also be done through relating myths. A god is what he does, and what he has done. Mentioning these myths not only honors him by telling of his wondrous deeds, it prepares him for the sort of request (if any) that is to follow. A prayer to Indra might begin, "Wielder of the vajra, slayer of Vrtra." This calls upon Indra as the keeper of the thunderbolt, the vajra, both the symbol and the means of operation of his power. Describing him as "slayer of Vrtra" defines Indra as the one who killed the great serpent in the beginning of time, removing the obstruction that kept the world from growing. This may hint at what you are about to ask for; perhaps there is some obstruction in your life that you would like removed. If you're praying to praise the god, it becomes something for which he should be honored. If you're praying out of gratitude, it expresses in a metaphor the kind of thing you are thanking him for.

Germanic literature uses an interesting means of relating these myths and titles called "kenning." In kenning, short descriptions can take the place of names or nouns, expressing a whole myth in a few words. For instance, Thor, who is to kill the wolf Fenrir in the battle at the end of time, would be called "Fenrir's Bane." This sort of allusion can bring in many myths in a short time, making a prayer multi-layered, and sending the worshipper's mind soaring outward into the divine realm by filling it with more than it can hold and forcing it to expand into a new spiritual reality.

In fact, it may not even be necessary to use the deity's name. Sometimes a myth or title is enough. There is no other deity who can be described as "Wielder of the vajra, slayer of Vrtra" except Indra. Remember, too, that what we think of as the names of the gods are sometimes titles by which they have become commonly known: Cernunnos is "The god with antlers," Epona is "The horse goddess," Mithra is "Contract." Sometimes these names are transparent to the worshipper, and sometimes they were devised so long ago that their meaning has been lost to their worshippers. I doubt that there was any ancient Greek who knew that Zeus meant "Bright Sky." But I'll bet Zeus knew, and when he was called upon by name, he knew that name was originally a title. Of course a name and its meaning, expressing a title, may coexist in one prayer. You can mix them together to get something like, "Great Mithra, Lord of Contract."

While it is true that myths can be used to identify a deity, it is also true that a prayer can actually relate a myth. The Homeric Hymns do this; they are, for instance, the main source for our knowledge of the myth of Demeter and Persephone. The telling can be the whole point of the myth, serving as praise, since everyone likes to have their deeds remembered. It can also teach both the person praying and anyone else present something about the deity addressed. Even if the story is known to all present, a good myth reveals something new each time it is told.

Identifying Deities by Their Titles

Titles can express the many sides of a deity. Most of us learned the job descriptions of the Greek and Roman gods when we were young—Venus was the goddess of love, Mars was the god of war, Mercury was the messenger of the gods. But gods are not that simple. Apollo, for instance, whom most of us learned to identify as the god of the Sun (and then we wondered how Helios could also be the god of the Sun) is god of music, beauty, order, and healing as well. Calling on him under these various areas of expertise rounds him out, makes him more real to us. For instance, a prayer to Apollo can begin, "I pray to the one whose arrows bring health and illness, to Apollo the beautiful one. From your lyre come tunes of harmonious enchantment, and I listen enraptured, sweet-singing Apollo."

Names, titles, their meanings, myths—you can mix them all together to define the recipient of your prayer more precisely: "Athena, Goddess of Wisdom, Protector of the crafty Odysseus." With each descriptive element, the deity becomes clearer in your mind, and you become more ready to open yourself to the holy presence.

The Ambiguity of the Gods

From the fact that gods are deeply three-dimensional comes one of their most important characteristics: ambiguity. They come to us at times that are neither one time nor another, such as dusk or dawn. They come to us in space that is neither one place nor another, such as tidal regions. And they come to us through actions that are neither one kind nor another, such as holding out our hands—are we giving, receiving, or both?

Thus we arrive at a seeming contradiction. Should you be precise in whom you call, taking care to invoke just the right aspect of your chosen deity? Or should you take care to preserve the ambiguity of the divine beings? There is really no problem here. Prayers have the same primary goal as other forms of communication—accuracy. What exactly are you trying to convey? Do you have one particular goal in mind? Then be precise. Are you interested in experiencing deities in all of their subtleties? Then be ambiguous.

Some deities are more ambiguous than others, of course. Hermes may be said to have ambiguity as his very nature, and gods such as Cernunnos, who have both an animal and a human nature, are implicitly ambiguous.

All gods have something about them that cannot quite be defined, however. If we could define them completely, we would limit them to such an extent that they would no longer be gods.

Prayers may effectively use ambiguity to express the nature of the gods. For instance, "Worthy are you of sacrifice" may mean either that the deity is worth sacrificing to or worth being sacrificed himself. The Wiccan God may appropriately be addressed in this way. Ambiguity is also useful for economy of language. It is the nature of symbols that they can have more than one meaning, and a prayer in which all of a symbol's meanings are used can be, in essence, several prayers at once.

Finally, the world is not simple. We do not always know the precise meaning of things, especially when the gods are involved. By speaking to our deities in ambiguous language, we remind both them and ourselves of this fact.

After naming your deities, mentioning their titles, and linking them with their myths, you can expand your identification by bringing up past favors, given either to you or to others: "Indra who slew the serpent, whose vajra has been ever my aid, who has been my steadfast companion." This links your identification with what comes next—either petition, praise, or thanksgiving.

Honoring Your Deities

You should do one last thing before you bring up the purpose of your prayer. You should honor your deity. (Of course, that might be the whole point of the prayer, and if so, good for you.) This is, at the very least, the polite thing to do. It also puts you into a proper relationship with your deity. The gods are more powerful than we are—more glorious, possessing more wisdom—and this should be recognized. In my own prayers, I prefer a simple: "I offer you my worship," or "I do you honor," or "I praise you, I honor you, I worship you."

If your prayer is one of praise, this pattern can be repeated over and over, building praise upon praise, until an ecstatic state of awareness of the deity is achieved. This can be followed by a period of silent contemplation, ending with a statement of gratitude.

Only after you have identified your deities, described them, linked yourself with them, and done them honor is it time to bring up your own intentions. If your prayer is one of thanksgiving, now is the time to offer your thanks. This is a good time to make an offering, either one promised earlier or one built into the prayer out of sheer gratitude: "I pour out this wine, Asklepios, for you have cured my illness." If the offering is in payment of a vow, that should be mentioned. A touching statement of faith from ancient times comes from the Roman practice of vowing to set up an altar when a prayer is answered. Hundreds of these have survived, each inscribed with a prayer of thanks: "[Name] dedicates this to [deity's name] willingly and deservingly in fulfillment of a vow." In fact, if your prayer asks for something, it is a good idea either to offer something at its end, or promise something upon the receipt of that which is asked. A gift demands a gift.

Exactly what gift to give will vary with the deity. There are deities associated with cows, such as Brighid or Juno; milk is a good gift for them. An appropriate offering for a storm god like Indra might be an axe, either actual or in miniature. Offerings can be based on your deity's culture; Roman gods like wine. If you can't decide what to give, stick to the basics: bread and a drink.

Composing Your Prayers

As you read through the prayers in this book, you'll find that I don't stick to the "pattern" described here very strictly. I generally use a few lines to set up the prayer, then I describe the situation addressed by the prayer. Only then do I begin to work within this pattern. I do this for a number of reasons.

First, there is not much point in using the pattern over and over. The suggestions given above and a few examples should be enough to enable you to write your own prayers. Second, prayers written in this other way have a built-in sacred space-and-time element. Before getting to the main purpose of the prayer, you define just where and when the prayer is being said. In that way, even if you have not established sacred space or time through ritual, you are nonetheless there. This can be a great help if you are in a situation where a full-fledged introductory ritual cannot be performed. It can even be useful if you do perform an introductory ritual, because that ritual is general. The first few lines of your prayers can then make the time and space more specific, focusing on the actual purpose of your prayer.

Not all prayers, or even all parts of a given prayer, are necessarily expressed in the first person: "I praise you," "I pray to Sarasvati." Third person prayers are also common:

Inanna rules over the gods.
She descends to death,
she ascends to life.
Neither death nor life can hold her.

This sort of prayer is great for praise, since you keep yourself out of the prayer, speaking only of the gods, describing them and their great deeds. By remembering them, you grow closer to them. This pleases them. Everyone wins. After speaking in the third person, you can then switch to the more expected format:

The spirits of the mountain exist in strength.
Their roots are deep in the Earth,
their heads pierce the air and mount to the sky above.
They dance from flat to peak
and, spiraling, descend again.
Good Ones, when I come under your trees and upon
your stones,
guide me.

In this case, you can think of the section spoken in the third person as both calling and praise. The gods come to hear of their deeds, delighting in them as a lord in a hall enjoys hearing his exploits sung before assembled guests. Then, when they have been pleased and are in a good mood, you can feel free to ask them for something. Or you can praise or thank them, shifting from an impersonal account of their greatness into a description of why they mean something to you, or how they have helped you. This sort of prayer recognizes both that the Holy Ones have concerns other than you and that you are concerned with them.

Litanies and Mantras

There are two types of prayers that do not necessarily fit into any of these formats: litanies and mantras. A litany is a call and response. It is, thus, appropriate for group practice. One person calls out something, and the others answer with a short prayer. For instance:

> *Queen of Stars*
> **we pray to you.**
>
> *Mother of All*
> **we pray to you.**

The words "we pray to you" in this example are the response. Litanies work really well for callings and praise. The repetition often leads to an ecstatic trance state; the back and forth of the calling and response gives a rhythm that adds to the effect.

Litanies can have a single leader for the whole prayer, or celebrants can sit in a circle and each person in turn can contribute a call. I don't recommend the latter because instead of concentrating on the litany, celebrants are trying to think of something to say when their turn comes. It is generally better if only one person is so distracted.

Mantras have a different structure. In a few lines (four is about the maximum), they sum up the essence of a deity and perhaps a desire of the person praying. For instance, the god Osiris (the Greek form of the Egyptian "Asar") is killed and dismembered. The pieces of his body are reassembled by his wife, Isis, and he becomes the lord of the dead. A mantra for him might be:

> *Asar slain and Asar living,*
> *Lord of death and of rebirth.*

Mantras are repeated many times. In fact, they can be repeated so often that, after a while, they become automatic, forming a background to your life. It is important that they have a rhythm so they can do this; an arrhythmic mantra is a distraction, requiring constant attention.

In some religions, such as Hinduism, there is a belief that certain sounds perfectly express certain truths. Repetition of these sounds, especially aloud, evokes their truths, which can be the nature of a divinity. If you accept the belief that sounds have this kind of power, I recommend you research the tradition you are drawn to and find out what mantras it uses. It is unlikely that you will stumble onto one that expresses just what you want it to express on your own. In general, however, it is quite possible that the names or titles of deities, in their original language, will function in this way. Even if they don't, they will be effective in other ways.

How do mantras work? They can serve to keep you constantly aware of the attributes of a deity. The more you repeat a mantra, the deeper an understanding you achieve of that deity's nature. This doesn't always happen in a conscious way. The awareness may percolate in your unconscious for some time; then, all of a sudden, you have an "aha!" experience, a flash of insight comes to you, seemingly from out of nowhere. Then you can return to your mantra with a new outlook.

Repeating a mantra can serve as constant praise. Over and over, you can send out words that recite your deity's deeds. In this way, the deity remains aware of your attention, which, is in itself, a form of praise.

Mantras are especially good for making certain contact with a deity. It can sometimes seem hard to reach the gods. They may be testing you, or you may not be in a state to receive or understand them. If the first is true, a mantra will show just how much you desire contact; if the second, repetition of the mantra will move you into a track along which you may approach the deity.

I myself have trouble feeling the immediate presence of a deity. I am very much a "head person," and opening myself up to a deity is very hard for me. It was more than a year before Cernunnos revealed himself to me. During that time, I took my usual approach, thinking about him constantly, turning things over in my mind. It eventually worked, and today I am very close to him. But it still took over a year.

Contrast this with my experience with Brighid. I used the mantra, "The fire of Brighid is the flame in my heart." I was working in retail at the time and, during slow periods, I would walk around the store repeating the mantra to myself. Within a few days, I could feel the goddess filling me completely; she was there and no doubt about it. Now Brighid is a deity who is very close to humanity, while Cernunnos is more aloof. Nonetheless, when you compare a year of mental effort to a few days of using a mantra, it's hard not to see the value of this kind of prayer.

Rosaries

A rosary can be used with a mantra. The rosary is most closely associated with Christianity, but it has been used by a number of other religions as well. I myself have used one for many years as part of my devotions to Nuit, the Thelemic goddess of infinite space. A rosary is simply a number of beads strung together with some space between them. You keep track of the number of prayers you say by moving your fingers along the beads. There is a large bead or some other marker to tell you when you have gone once around. The exact number of beads (and thus of prayers) is up to you. You can make it appropriate in some way to the deity to whom you are praying or to some aspect of your religious tradition.

For instance, my Nuit rosary had five groups of eleven beads each, each group separated by two slightly larger beads. The numbers five and eleven are significant to Nuit. The total number of small beads was thus fifty-five. The large bead at the end (which had its own prayer) made fifty-six beads—another significant number. The dividing beads, again with the large bead, were eleven. A Wiccan rosary might have thirteen beads, for the lunar months in a year, or twenty-eight, for the days in a lunar month. A Celtic rosary might be arranged in three groups of nine. And so on.

You don't have to have a physical rosary. I used to sometimes say my Nuit rosary lying in bed at night, my fingers counting the prayers under my pillow. By tightening one finger at a time, one hand would count out eleven prayers—one for each finger in one direction, one for each back, and a final tightening of the whole hand. My other hand kept track of how many times I had gone through the cycle of eleven. With a system like this, you can count prayers almost anywhere.

Keeping track of the number of times you run through a rosary can be a problem. After all, the main reason for using a rosary is to count without having to pay attention. Catholics keep track of the number of passes by meditating on the mysteries of the Church, a different one for each cycle.

You can use a similar system. For instance, if you are a Wiccan with a twenty-eight-bead rosary, go through it thirteen times, each time thinking of a different Moon in the year. (In many systems, each Moon has a name.) Once you have completed all thirteen Moons, add a final prayer $((28 \times 13) + 1 = 365)$, and you will have gone through a year. In other traditions, you can devise a similar system.

Ending Prayers

When you finish a prayer, you may feel a need to say something to cap it off—an "amen." Something seems necessary, if only to keep the prayer from drifting off into nothingness. In public prayer, a firm ending also gives those present who may not have said anything a chance to add their own prayer by assenting to the one that has already been made.

Many Wiccans use the Masonic "so mote it be." Many Pagans use the American Indian "Ho." Each has its own disadvantage. The first is ponderous, and the second can be seen as "playing Indian."

How about "amen"? It's Hebrew for "so be it," and, with the deep associations it has within many of our psyches with prayer, it is a fine ending. The objection will, of course, be made that it is Judaeo-Christian. That may be so, but the phrase long ago made its way into our culture in a manner that transcends its original religious meaning. "God," "deity," and "heaven" all come from non-Christian roots, yet these words have been enthusiastically embraced by Christians. We can do the same with this lovely little word—amen.

Choosing Words for Prayer

The actual words you use in a prayer matter. Each word has a number of meanings assigned to it—the denotative meaning (what it technically means), the connotative meaning (how people feel about it), and the meaning that arises from the sound. For instance, "break" can mean "time off from work." That is its denotative meaning. It has a strongly positive connotation, since we all like breaks (that's why we take them). And it ends with a strong stop, expressing the idea of a cut between one state and another. A good prayer will try to harmonize all three kinds of meaning. Fortunately, English has a huge vocabulary (about a million words), so you can usually find a word that expresses exactly the meaning you want.

The economy of language that is found in prayers is sometimes given as the definition of poetry. It is certainly true that many prayers are in the form of poetry; most of them in this book are. This is partially an artificial effect, however, because prayers such as these are formal, and formal prayers benefit from poetic structure. In particular, poetry is easier to memorize than prose, and it is easier to say smoothly as well.

In a poem, not only the words convey meaning, but also the structure. A well-ordered poetic prayer expresses the nature of an orderly god, such as Zeus or Apollo. A poem can even be discordant, with random meters, suggesting a deity of disorder, such as Eris.

When you wish to set a prayer in the form of a poem, you can use all the characteristics of poetry. The characteristic most people think of when poetry is mentioned is rhyme. Good rhyme is very difficult to write (when I do it, it usually ends up sounding like a bad greeting card). If you can do it, however, it can be quite effective. Rhyme joins the lines of a poem together, making it into a connected whole. In a prayer, that means that each line reinforces the others, increasing the meaning of the prayer.

One of the reasons rhyme is so effective is that it reinforces another basic quality of poetry—rhythm. Rhyming is, itself, a rhythm. A prayer can have rhythm without rhyming, however. Robert Graves described the natural rhythm of English as "the pulling of an oar." Reading good poetry aloud can teach you to feel the natural rhythm of the words. Shakespeare's soliloquies are good works to use for this.

If you have studied poetry, you have come across words that describe different meters, terms like "iambic pentameter." I must admit that these terms have defied all my attempts to memorize them, and I wouldn't dream of trying to explain them to you. Fortunately, I don't have to; any introductory text on poetry will do that. More important than the technical terms for meter is the feel of the words anyway. Experiment with different patterns of words and see what kind of effect they have on you.

One interesting poetic technique that is fairly easy to use is alliteration. This consists simply of using words that start with the same letter: "the silent storm still approaches." This technique can tie sentences into a single unit. Germanic poetry uses a lot of alliteration. It breaks sentences in two; one half contains two alliterating words, and the other half contains one or two more. These words have to be stressed words—words containing an accented syllable—and the stressed syllable is the one that alliterates. "From the great sea's foam, a fish is flung."

Another technique is repetition. This can be exact: "Lord of the Pathway, to you I call; Lord of the Pathway, who crushes obstructions." It can consist of parallel meaning, rather than a repetition of the exact words: "Gods of the Ancients, to you I call; in my hour of need, I lift my voice to you." And the two can also be combined: "Lord of the Pathway, to you I call; Lord of the Pathway, I lift my voice to you."

Like rhythm, rhyme, and alliteration, repetition ties a prayer together. In fact, all these techniques serve to make the prayer more than a random collection of words. They make it a single unit, with one purpose. This purpose will differ from prayer to prayer, but, in any single prayer, there is one single purpose to which the entire prayer is bent.

Set Prayers and Spontaneous Prayers

I do not think that even the most hard-nosed proponent of set prayers would be opposed to spontaneous prayer. The techniques given in this chapter are meant to teach you how to compose your own prayers. Once you have mastered them, you can compose prayers anywhere, anytime. If you follow these rules, your prayers will be no less spontaneous than your normal speech is when you follow the rules of grammar. They may even help to make your prayers more spontaneous, since having some order to rely on sometimes opens us up creatively. On the other hand, even if you don't use these techniques, you can impress the gods with your sincerity by speaking what you truly feel.

The disagreement arises when people oppose set prayers on principle. Their attitude seems to be that a prayer must come from the heart; it must be completely unique to the moment, expressing what the person praying feels at just that point in time. Anything else is thought to be insincere. I understand this position. It goes with a search for authenticity, for truth in all things. That is a principle I can get behind. I just don't think it has anything to do with the legitimacy of set prayers.

In many cases, this attitude is, itself, not authentic. Neo-Paganism is cursed with a number of problems that have their roots in the childhood practices and beliefs of its members. Since they belong to a religion formed mainly of converts (a situation that is, fortunately, now changing), neo-Pagans have a bad tendency to react against their early religious background, which, in most cases, is Christianity. They seem to believe that Christianity is a religion of rote repetition, whereas Paganism is, by nature, spontaneous.

This does both Christianity and Paganism a disservice. The repetition of a memorized prayer is not necessarily a mechanical thing. It involves a relationship between the pray-er, the prayer, and the one prayed to. This relationship is expressed through the words of a prayer, perhaps, but each prayer event is no more identical to those before than each performance of a particular piece of music is the same as another.

Ancient Paganism, for its own part, had set prayers. The *Rig Veda* is a collection of prayers that acquired canonical status. In Pagan Rome, following set prayers was so important that an assistant with a prayer book stood next to priests, whispering the proper words to them. There is, thus, definitely a strong Pagan tradition of set prayers.

And why shouldn't there be? Our circumstances aren't that much different from those of others—we mourn, feel gratitude, desire to praise, want to make requests. Why should each of us have to compose a prayer each time we need one? I happen to be good at writing prayers. I'm a lousy plumber. If there is a plumber out there who isn't good at writing prayers, why shouldn't we avail ourselves of each other's talents?

Most important of all, there are times when we want to pray, but words fail us. I think here of mourners at a Catholic funeral praying the rosary. Locked in their grief, they fix their minds on words they know by heart. They no longer need to think; they give themselves over to mourning and are comforted. It would be a shame for Pagans not to have the same gift.

Moreover, it is impossible for people to pray spontaneously as a group. They need to know what to say, so they can say it together. Prayer is not just a private matter. Sometimes a group will be drawn together by circumstances—anything from a funeral to a seasonal celebration—and they will want to pray together. Sometimes, the whole point of praying will be to practice religious acts as a group. Prayer can be used to unify people; those who say the same words are, in a sense, one. The Catholic mourners described above can know that the other mourners are feeling the same thing they are, and be comforted by that.

The most important rationale for set prayers, however, is a phenomenon I call "deepening." The more often a prayer is said, the deeper it sinks into your consciousness. Eventually, it sinks into your unconscious mind. When this happens, it can be said that the prayer prays you. It becomes part of who you are. It changes you in a way that would not have been possible with a prayer said once and forgotten.

It should come as no surprise, of course, that I like set prayers. This is, after all, a book of them. I have given you quite a few to work with here. I have also shown you how to write your own. If you do write your own prayers, don't discard them after use. Work with them more than once. Chew them over in your mind; let them grow in you. You will discover an amazing thing—you have written better than you had thought. As the prayer is said on each new occasion, you will discover insights in it that you didn't even know were there. It is an amazing feeling. I would hate for you to be deprived of it.

When you feel as though nothing will do but to burst forth with a prayer, go right ahead. Don't feel as if you're cheating either the gods or yourself, however, if what comes forth is a pre-learned prayer. Sometimes set prayers can carry meaning even better than those you come up with on the spur of the moment.

PART II

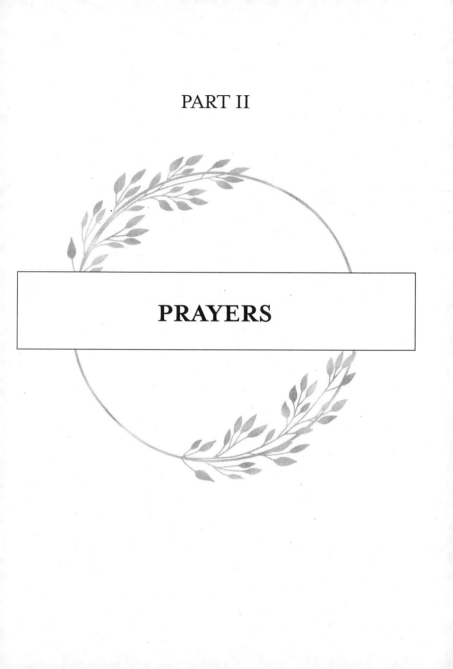

PRAYERS

CHAPTER 5

PRAYERS FOR THE FAMILY AND THE HOUSEHOLD

Worship in the home is the most important of Pagan practices. The great festivals come and go, the Moon turns round, the Sun rises and sets, but their celebrations are done against the background of home worship.

Home worship is made up of those practices through which the deities, Ancestors, and spirits who preside over the family and protect the home are worshipped, honored, and propitiated. Long sentence. More precisely, there are divine beings of various sorts who watch over a family and its home, and they like to be recognized. We do this, as usual, through prayers and offerings.

Spirits of Place

The main sacred places of a household where worship is performed are the hearth and the threshold. If the home stands on its own property, the yard and the property's border are also sacred. Each of these places has its own spirits, and traditional ways to honor them.

The hearth was originally the multi-purpose fireplace—it cooked our meals, warmed our homes, and boiled water for washing. Although today these functions have been split up between the stove, the furnace, and the water heater, they are no less sacred, and no less worthy of honor. There is a spirit living in the hearth of each home; in fact, most likely that spirit is a great goddess, perhaps the most important of the goddesses, since she is the heart of the home and the home is the heart of our lives.

You should honor this goddess primarily at the stove, since that is where our nourishment—that which fuels our own inner fires—is prepared. Keep a candle or oil lamp next to the stove, and light it when you pray to her. Don't forget to honor her at the furnace or water heater, though.

At least once a year, on a day appropriate to your deity, make special offerings at each of them. For instance, honor Brighid on February 2nd (Brighid's Day) and Vesta on June 9th (Vestalia). Alternatively, you could choose the anniversary of the day you moved in.

The threshold is a place particularly appropriate for worship. It marks a point of transition between one place and another. These in-between places throb with power; they are like circuits formed through the flow between positive and negative forces. Like electricity, their power can help or harm. The purpose of threshold devotions is to make sure that the positive forces are directed to family and friends, and the harmful ones to intruders.

The yard is a place where wild things can roam in safety and do you no harm. By letting them move about on your "turf," but outside, you give them a secure haven and ensure your own safety as well. Here you can approach the outside world and introduce yourself to it, while still keeping one foot securely inside your home. Many spirits roam this outdoor space, and all are worthy of prayer and praise.

The boundary line of your property is the threshold of your household world, and has the same meanings that your house's threshold has. It is where that which is yours finally ends, and the common area begins. It is where you must say goodbye to the familiar. When you do, ask for one last blessing from your household spirits by praying to the spirit of the border. You can also ask that your border spirit prevent anything harmful from entering your property while you are away.

Patron Deities and Ancestors

Besides the spirits of place, there are deities who watch over individual members of your household. These are the patron deities mentioned earlier. Worshipping them should be part of your home practice. There are too many deities, each with their own worship requirements, to cover them all here. Suffice it to say that the usual rules for prayer and offering given in Part I apply for these deities as well—purification is good, fire is great, prayers have a traditional structure, and everybody likes presents.

Just as a house has its protective spirits, and individual members of the family have their patron deities, so too the family as a whole has its protectors. These are the Ancestors. In the case of the family worship, they are the genetic ancestors, those who founded the family and those who kept it going. Of course, families can grow by adoption as well as reproduction, so those who are adopted into a family are adopted into the line of its Ancestors as well.

Many of our ancestors would be appalled to learn that we are praying to them. At least, that's how they would probably have felt when they were alive. But they're dead now, and we can hope that their perspective has changed, that they have acquired the wisdom granted by distance. Even if they don't want worship, technically we are honoring them rather than worshipping them, and they can't mind that much.

Somewhere in your home, by the hearth, or in the entranceway, or on a kitchen shelf, you should have a shrine. In it, put images of the patron deities of the members of your household, images of the Ancestors, and a source of fire (a candle or oil lamp). Images can be statues or more abstract. My wife's patron is Venus, and for a long time, I used a star-shaped stone (making it also roughly the shape of a person) that I had found on the seashore as her image. An antler can serve as an image of Cernunnos, a mirror as one of Amaterasu. Ancestors can be represented by generic statues of a man and a woman. This shrine provides the divine beings most closely associated with your home with their own place in it. The fire, which represents divinity, both honors them and is a means to contact them. It is here that you should pray and make offerings to these protective beings.

Water and Fire

Before beginning your household rituals, it's good to call on those most holy of things, water and fire. In many other cases, you may have to pray without them, but in your own home, you have them ready at hand. Purify yourself with the water, and then light the fire. A short prayer such as "I light the fire of offering" would be nice. If you are honoring your hearth deity, you will want to light *her* flame, with a short prayer such as "I light the fire of [her name]." There is no need to establish sacred space. A home is by nature a sacred space.

If you are praying to the threshold, yard, or border spirits, go to where they dwell. Leave the fire burning in your shrine during the ritual, though. It is your anchor.

When you make offerings indoors, such as to the hearth, make them into a bowl. If you can, leave them there for twenty-four hours and then take them outside for the Land Spirits to eat. Offerings to land and border spirits can usually be made right on the spot. In the case of a threshold, if your door opens to the outside, liquid offerings can be made right on it. If your door opens out, put your offerings in a bowl right inside the door and dispose of them as usual.

Remember that you pray with deeds as well as words. Not stepping on your threshold as you come in or go out can be a prayer. With time, it will become a habit; your conscious mind will not notice, but with your unconscious mind, you will be praying.

Traditional Roles

Household prayers may be said by any member of the family (and if you live alone, you will, of course, be doing all of it by yourself). Traditionally, however, certain people had certain responsibilities. Maintaining these traditions will put you more strongly in tune with your Ancestors.

The worship of the hearth goddess was the responsibility of the wife and mother in ancient times. The father was responsible for performing the rest of the family worship on his family's behalf. He was, in other words, the priest of the family.

You don't have to stick to these roles. The spirits like to be remembered, no matter who is doing the remembering. As the main cook in my house, I've been the one to maintain the hearth-goddess worship. You can share these responsibilities in whatever way seems fit for your family. Assign some duties to your children as they grow. Learning not to step on the threshold is something that can be done as soon as a child can walk. Honoring their own patrons is something that should be taught to children early as well.

A distinction can be made between the prayers of family members to the household spirits and prayers to the spirits on the family's behalf. Someone should be doing the latter. This is enough, but it is very basic. It is good if all members of the family, as individuals, are in a right relationship with the household spirits. This relationship exists alongside the one each person has with a personal patron deity. Through the worship of a patron deity, each person is established as an individual; through the worship of the household spirits, each person is established as a member of a family.

Household Prayers

The different domestic deities can be worshipped together, or separately. Here are some examples of such prayers.

> *Goddess of the hearth, beat strong and pure in the*
> *heart of my home.*
> *Lord of the threshold, keep vigilant guard over the*
> *entrance to my home.*
> *Spirits of the land, keep watch throughout the yard*
> *of my home.*
> *God of the borders, stand ready to repulse all*
> *disorder from my home.*

Prayers to the Hearth Goddess

The following prayers can be addressed to the goddess of your own hearth. Where appropriate, you can substitute the name of your own hearth deity, of course.

> *Fire softly glowing in the heart of my home,*
> *Goddess of the hearth, life of my dwelling,*
> *keep my family free from discord,*
> *free from want, free from fear,*
> *free from all that would disturb us*
> *and that would disturb your perfect peace.*

☽ ○ ☾

> *The fire from the waters is here.*
> *The fire from the land is here.*
> *The fire from the sky is here.*

From below, from about, from above,
Fire has come here to my hearth:
Burn there, Lady of Clear Sight.

[Water (below), land (about), and sky (above) are the traditional realms of many cultures, especially the Indo-European. This is a prayer for lighting your hearth flame.]

☽ ○ ☾

A burning point are you, Lady.
A center point are you, Lady.
A place of light are you, Lady.
A place of warmth are you, Lady.
The heart of our home are you, Lady.

☽ ○ ☾

To you, Fiery One, I give this milk;
I pour it out in your honor.

[Offerings to a hearth deity should be homey consumables, such as milk, bread, or butter. Wine is too fancy, mead a bit affected. Beer isn't bad, though.]

Brighid

The home's central point is a glowing fire,
the heart of our home shining brightly.
Brighid, Queen of Fire, bless all of your people,
all who dwell in this house.

[You can substitute the name of your own hearth deity, of course.]

Vesta

> **Vesta, eat what is offered to you**
> **and transform it, as food is transformed,**
> **into blessings for me, and for all my household.**

The next two prayers can be said each time you light a fire in a fireplace, but they are just as good for re-lighting a pilot light when you move into a new home. With "wood" changed to "oil," the first prayer is equally good for an oil lamp.

> **The fire that burns on my hearth is the very heart of**
> **my home.**
> **By feeding the fire with wood and with air, I am**
> **feeding my home with what it needs most.**
> **I give you these things, fire on my hearth and more**
> **gifts will follow as we live our lives together.**

☽ ○ ☾

> **I light a fire on my family's hearth and praise the**
> **gods of our home.**
> **I burn incense to the High Ones and pour out**
> **libations to the Ancestors.**
> **Hear my words, see me as I perform the rites, receive**
> **the gifts I offer to you.**

Prayers to the Threshold Spirits

> **Threshold Spirit, guardian and protector of my**
> **house's entrance,**
> **I honor you as I pass through the door.**

Janus

Janus, god of doorways,
bless my goings out,
bless my comings in.

[Touch the door post reverently as you say this. You can say it each time you leave your house, or when you leave it for the first time each day.]

☽ ○ ☾

Lord of the threshold,
of doors and gates lord,
place where inside and outside meet:
Janus is my threshold.

☽ ○ ☾

Guard my door, Janus,
keeper of the keys.
Watch it with care,
keep my home safe.

☽ ○ ☾

May the blessings of Janus guard this door.
Janus it is who guards our doors.

[This prayer is appropriate for when you are locking up for the night.]

Prayers to the Spirits of the Yard

The yard spirits are half wild, and their actions are not always what we would wish. This is especially true when they are ignored. Give them the leavings of your offerings to the inside spirits to them, as well as an offering of their own, such as a piece of buttered bread, from time to time. And remember, no matter how reassuring order may be, it can be a bit oppressive. Try to keep part of your yard, even a back corner, as a haven for the wild. Leave it alone, let weeds grow there, and don't mow it. Give the spirits who live there occasional offerings. Leave the offerings there until they are gone. Is the milk eaten by the spirits, washed away by rain, or lapped up by a wandering cat? Who knows? Who cares? Perhaps the spirits have come in the form of rain or a cat. It doesn't matter. What matters is that you do the right thing. In this case, having a piece of the wild in the midst of your tame yard will bring you a bit of the wildness and peace that the wild can bring.

Roam about our land at will, spirits,
keeping it holy by your presence.

☽ ○ ☾

Guardians of rocks and trees,
of grass and garden,
of wild places and tame,
of outbuildings and outside:
be benevolent to us,
to those who tend your realm,
and we will be benevolent to you.

☽ ○ ☾

A piece of wild on the edge of the tame,
you are home to wild spirits who live with us.
You who live here, be pleased with this offering.
Give us a piece of the wild to keep us alive and fresh.

Prayers to the Border Spirits

A householder is responsible for all who dwell in the house, but especially for guests. Treat anyone who has safely passed the borders of your land with respect, unless they perform some act that offends the household spirits. Even then, treat them with kindness until you have escorted them off your property. It is then your responsibility to patch things up with whatever spirits have been offended. This obligation holds for the uninvited as well as the invited guest—the neighborhood children, the salesman, the evangelist at your door. Greet them pleasantly. Offer them hospitality. If you invite them in, offer them something to eat or drink. Your home will develop a reputation for hospitality, which will please the household spirits no end.

He who sits at the edge of my land
sits at the edge of all I own.
Watchful Terminus guards my space.

☽ ○ ☾

About my house, establish your place of warding.
Stand watchfully at the corners.
Be a shield between our house and all that would
work evil.
Guard our land and all who claim its protection.

Here on the border, you stand your watch. I have
come out here to assure you that your attention
to duty is appreciated, bringing not only words,
but gifts to place before your marker. Watcher on
the Borders, the steward of this land offers to you.
This grain is for you, and this beer is for you.

Prayers to the Ancestors

Samhain is the day on which the ancient Celts honored their
ancestors, and many neo-Pagans have adopted it for this
purpose. Most cultures have such a day, and you should use
whatever one is right for your ancestry. If you are, like so
many of us, of mixed ancestry, Memorial Day makes a nice
compromise.

I have chanted your names each Samhain as is my
duty.
I have offered thanksgiving gifts for the births of my
children, as is only right.
I have not forgotten where I came from, and have
kept the old ways, as is only proper.
I therefore turn in confidence to you, spirits of my
Ancestors,
and ask your protection for my family and all its
property.

☽ ○ ☾

The ground on which we stand,
the starter block of our race;[1]
the slate on which we write,
the pattern behind our lives.
You who lived in the times before us,
who laid down the way on which we travel,
who established traditions that guide our people,
whose blood flows red within us,
whose genes have engendered us:
a gift for you, a small one in return
for the great ones you have given us.
Even the greatest, life itself, is your gift to us.
A gift, then, from life to the dead.

☽ ○ ☾

Old Ones who grace our shrine,
who grace our line,
who grace our lives:
we honor you with right living,
making you proud of us;
the best offering you could receive.
But today a small offering, a token.

CHAPTER 6

CALLINGS

Callings serve two purposes. First, they do just what the name implies: they call out to deities. They let them know we have need of them. Our deities are not omniscient; they take part in the world, rather than stand outside it. They are, thus, subject to limitations. If we want their presence, we have to call them, like children calling for their parents in the night. The demand is based on love, and parents respond to it.

There is also an element of responsibility at work here. Parents are responsible for their children, and so will respond to their calls. The gods know they have more power than we do, and this gives them a certain responsibility. They will help us, because they know it is right for them to do so.

Second, callings prepare us to receive our deities. They set up a relationship through which the gods may come to us. And they prepare us so that, when the gods come, we will see them.

Callings do *not*, however, force the deities to come. Prayers do not invoke with all-powerful names. They reach out and ask the gods to reach back.

Sometimes the best way to call a deity is simply to keep silent and let the deity arrive. And if prayer is a conversation with divine beings, it is only right that we should occasionally let them speak too.

I sit still, that my motion may not hide your presence.
I do not speak, that my words may not hide your
    voice.
I will still my thoughts, that my thinking might not
    block your arrival.

[A general-purpose prayer, one that can be used for any deity with the addition of a line or two at the beginning: "Diana of the silver bow, riding the sky, hunting in the forests," "Wielder of the great weapons, Ba'al," "Agni, speaking in the fire's flaming."]

$$\text{☽ ◯ ☾}$$

Gods of old, long have you waited,
seemingly forgotten and outgrown,
waiting with the patience born of wisdom,
for your children to remember you
and to come to you with open hearts.
Awake, come, that day is here.
Once more we pour libations,
once more the old songs rise,
once more the dance steps are traced,
once more your names are spoken.
Never more will the altars be unattended.
Never again the time of waiting.
Your children look to you once again
and pledge to you their faith.

$$\text{☽ ◯ ☾}$$

Hail to you, mighty ones of old,
from ancient times till now your splendor endures.
We, your children, call out to you again;
as in the childhood of our race, we acknowledge our
*   debts.*
Deities of light and deities of darkness,
both gods and goddesses: we praise you.
Not forgetting one, not leaving any out,
we send our prayers to all of you.
Listen to our words; you will find them sweet.
Your children pray to you here.

☽ ○ ☾

Sitting in anticipation of their coming, I open my
*   mind to make their way smooth.*
May the gods hear what I say and answer me,
*   blessing me with their presence.*

☽ ○ ☾

Accept my hospitality, Holy Ones;
be my guests at this feast.
Renew the ancient bonds,
continually recreated.
As I give, so will you,
for that is how true friends act.
Great company of gods,
I welcome you.

[To accompany offerings given at a meal to which the gods are invited.]

☽ ○ ☾

I call to the Holy Ones with open hands
asking that they come, that they grant me their
presence.
Mighty and Shining Ones, worthy of worship,
I stand before you with welcoming words.
Come to me that we might feast together again.

$$\mathcal{D} \; O \; \mathbb{C}$$

With this small flame I send a message—
it is my burning beacon fire.
May you see it, Shining Ones,
and draw near to me.
Filled with the holy power the gods send to those
they love
I rise up in ecstasy, taken by them to the Land of
Blessings.
Fill me, carry me, lift me in glory;
welcome me to your home.

[This prayer is a little different. Instead of calling the gods to your world, it asks them to take you to theirs. You can repeat the words "welcome me to your home" until the desired feeling of ecstasy comes and you do indeed feel lifted up to the gods. Then, if you are up to it, you can add the last two lines.]

$$\mathcal{D} \; O \; \mathbb{C}$$

I pour out this libation to you, as has been done
since ancient times.
Come and accept your due.

$$\mathcal{D} \; O \; \mathbb{C}$$

Do you smell this?
Do you smell my incense as the smoke goes up in
your honor?
I am the one who waits for you,
praising you, even in your absence.
Do not withhold yourself from me,
from one who brings you gifts,
from one who awaits you patiently.

The God and the Goddess

Wicca is the most popular form of neo-Paganism. In its most basic form, Wicca has two deities—the God and the Goddess. All of the other gods and goddesses are considered manifestations of these two. In some versions of Wicca, the other deities are believed to have their own existence, but the God and Goddess are still seen as having the qualities of all the deities.

Since many non-Wiccan religions worship certain deities who have qualities similar to the God and Goddess, some of these prayers may fit them as well. The first gives the simplest form of a calling, and may be used for any deity merely by changing the name, and the sex if necessary.

The God

The Wiccan God is seen as the basis or chief of all the gods. He is associated with the Sun and sky, thought of as dying and reborn with the year, and often called "All Father." The first prayer may also be used by a group as

a litany, with "Come to us, Lord" being used as a refrain
after each line.

Like a lightning flash cleaving the night,
Like the sun rising inexorably over the horizon,
Like a stone exploding amongst the flames,
Like an arrow seeking its prey in the forest:
Come to me, Lord.
Like a roebuck breaking free from a thicket,
Like an eagle stooping with claws outstretched,
Like a wildfire consuming tree after tree,
Like a hammer striking sparks against the anvil:
Come to me, Lord.
Like a thunderstorm opening up in summer heat,
Like an earthquake shaking the mountains,
Like a gale blowing across open water,
Like a cloud of spears showering down on a
*   battlefield:*
Come to me, Lord.

☽ ○ ☾

He it is who appears suddenly; he does not give me
*   time to prepare.*
And how would I prepare, anyway, against one such
*   as him?*
Nothing can withstand him, if that be his wish:
he is the unconquered one, the victor, inexorably
*   advancing.*
Lord of Radiance, I wait for you.
I will not resist.
Come like a blasting wind;
even then I will be here with mind open before you,

even then I will be here with heart open before you,
even then I will be here with hands open before you,
awaiting your coming.

☽ ○ ☾

You who wear the antlers:
both beast and man.
You accompanied by stag and dog:
both wild and tame.
You who sit upon the threshold:
both in and out.
You who are the Lord of the in-between:
to you I pray.

☽ ○ ☾

I am here, Lord, beneath your over-reaching dome,
calling to you from the world so far below you.
I send my words up to you, building a road on which
*   you might descend.*
See them there, glowing in the air, the straight road
*   leading to me.*
Come to me, I ask, guiding yourself by my prayer,
come without error, and without delay, to me.
Between us there is a bond, strengthened by the
*   thread of my prayer.*
Come to me, who worship you.
Come, answer my prayer.

☽ ○ ☾

Tell me, Lord, what your message is for me. I have
*   tried to decide for some time just what it is that*
*   you have to teach me. Now, at the end of my*

resources, I finally do what I should have done
first: ask you yourself. Speak to me, Lord, and I
will listen.

☽ ○ ☾

The Serpent King is stirring within me,
awakening, his fire and force growing.
The raving one awakes, who is spendthrift with his
*   power,*
breaking through, breaking down, breaking apart
*   what is outworn.*
Do what you must, thunder and lightning,
but leave behind a newly ordered creation,
an oak growing from the wet ground.

[This prayer, which invokes the God in an especially disturbing form,
would also be appropriate for a boy undergoing puberty. With the
replacement of "you" for "me" it could be said by the boy's father in
blessing.]

The Goddess

The Wiccan Goddess is seen as the basis of all goddesses.
She is often called the "All Mother," and is linked with both
the Earth and the Moon.

I pray to her who is the Mother of All
and ask her presence today.

☽ ○ ☾

Mari, Mater, Anna:
I call to you by these ancient names.

I call to you by these names you are known by
and ask you to come to me.

☽ ○ ☾

Wheels turn
and the seasons turn
and the earth turns
and the stars turn.
The universe turns
and I turn with it.
Queen of the turning,
my face turns toward you in wonder.

☽ ○ ☾

Great Mother, help me. I have studied your ways
for many years now, and still you hide yourself
from me. I can call to you under a multitude
of names, but still you do not come. I can tell a
large number of your stories, but still I do not
know who you are. I have many pictures of you,
but still I have not seen your face. Though I
throw out titles and powers and associations in
mad armfuls, still there is nothing there when
the whirlwind I create has become still. In that
nothing, then, in the quiet after my storm, I will
await you. Come to me, if such is your will, or do
not come to me, if such is your will. Still I will
wait. What else can I do?

The Gods

Most forms of Paganism are unashamedly polytheistic, believing in a multitude of deities. Hinduism alone traditionally believes in 330,000,000; I myself believe in an effectively infinite number, although I personally worship only a few. With so many gods to choose from, it is obvious that, in this and later sections, I will only be able to address some. I have, therefore, had to choose a subset from various types and traditions and cultures. For those deities not represented here, some of these prayers can be adapted, or at least serve as models or inspiration for your own.

I bring greetings to the gods of this place
from my people, from my family, from me,
and not only greetings but gifts of friendship.
I give them to you to establish between us the sacred
    bond.

☽ ○ ☾

I who stand before you,
I who come into your presence,
I who am your worshipper,
call out to you,
[   ].

God of the Pathway

Lord of the Pathway, to you I call;
Lord of the Pathway, I lift my voice to you.
Gate Keeper, Waiting One,

Open the door,
that I might pass through to the land of the Gods,
there to be refreshed by the power of the Great Ones.[1]

Amaterasu

Don't hide in your cave of clouds, Amaterasu,
and deprive our world of your splendor.
Come to the mirror we have prepared,
washing it with clear water.
See, we are clean too;
nothing is here which would defile.
We are worthy of your presence and eager to see you.
Leave your cloud cave and shine for us.

[There is a little ritual prescribed in this prayer. The person praying washes themselves. (Japanese deities are real sticklers for purity and cleanliness.) A mirror (the image of Amaterasu) is also washed, and set up in a shrine. The worshiper then bows and claps their hands before praying.]

Apollo

Apollo of the shining bow,
with hair of flame, with beauty shining,
truth's bright friend and falsehood's foe,
master of both lyre and singing:
Be with me, bring art and grace,
Be with me, bring light and song,
Be·with me, bring all that is beautiful,
bring all that is beautiful when you come to me.

Brighid

Come to us in the fire on our hearth;
consume the logs gladly.
Come to our home, Brighid of Protection;
consume the logs gladly.

☽ ○ ☾

Triple fire shining in the hearth of our home,
Brighid, Healer Brighid, to you our worship,
to you our hearts calling.
Triple flame burning in the hearth of our strength,
Brighid, Mighty Brighid, to you our worship,
to you our hearts calling.
Triple blaze leaping in the hearth of our souls,
Brighid, Poet Brighid, to you our worship,
to you our hearts calling
Triple tongue speaking, to you we listen.

Cernunnos

Be with me, Cernunnos,
whether I am moving or standing still,
whether at home or abroad,
whether at work or at rest.
Be my strength and my counselor,
providing both the judgment to choose the right path
and the courage to walk it boldly.

The Daghda

Daghda Mor, I speak your name,
Emptier of cauldrons, your child calls you:
into the past
through the mists
over the border between our worlds
my words go flying straight to you.
Eochu Ollathair, I speak your name,
Marker of borders, your child calls you:
out of the past
through the mists
over the border between our worlds
travel the trackway, straight to me.
Morrígan mate, hear my words.
Champion eater, receive my gift.

Dionysos

Dionysos, Lord of the Vine,
inhabiting spirit of the wine-filled cup,
bring joy to those who come together here.
Bind us together in the brotherhood of the cup.

☽ ○ ☾

You who fill your devotees with ecstasy
pouring yourself unreservedly through their lips,
I ask you for your presence here today
that our gathering might be properly blessed.

Dyḗus Ptḗr

May my prayer be the road on which you come
from your celestial home, Dyḗus Ptḗr.
May my words be food for your shining horses
as they carry you to me, Dyḗus Ptḗr.
Enter this space, guided by what I speak:
Come to one who is faithful to you,
Come to one who does not neglect his duties to you,
Come to one who is not stingy with offerings.
Dyḗus Ptḗr come to me.

☽ ○ ☾

I stand here on the summit of your high mountain,
and think of you.
Surrounded by the sky, lifted up into the sky itself,
the awesome clarity of your focused vision comes
closer to me
and I am more aware, myself, of your law's urgings.
Dyḗus Ptḗr, lord of all that is right, of all that is just,
of all that should be;
Dyḗus Ptḗr judge and king of the world, of all who
live and all that is,
Dyḗus Ptḗr advise me; make the right path open
beneath my feet,
make my eyesight clear, that I may always see as far
as I do from the top of this mountain of yours.

Gʷouwindā

Your outstretched enfolding arms offer cattle,
pour out rich milk,
that we might, like children, grow in prosperity.
Leading cows you come to your worshipers,
who, pouring golden butter, come to you.

Lugh

A flaming spear out of the chaos
Lugh Lamfhada, come to your people
A skillful hand against the chaos
Lugh Lamfhada, come to your people
A mind keenly ordered amidst the chaos
Lugh Lamfhada, come to your people
A faithful protector through all the chaos
Lugh Lamfhada, come to your people.
Dragon slayer, craftsman, singer and warrior,
Lugh Lamfhada, Lugh Lamfhada, Lugh Lamfadha,
Come to your people.

Nuit

Long is the hair of the Star Goddess
and long is the night in which I wait for her.
Lost in the expanse of limitless space
containing infinite numbers of stars but filled with
emptiness.
I cast myself into her measureless darkness,
confident that she will come if only I wait.

Though the night may be long, I will still wait for her,
offering my patience in sacrifice to win her presence.

[This would work for the Egyptian Nut as well. Since the Wiccan
Goddess is sometimes called "Star Goddess," it can even be used
for her.]

Rhiannon

On the edge of sight I can see a wonder:
a woman on a horse walking slowly away,
her moon-pale steed taking even strides.
If I send swift thoughts racing after her
I cannot overtake her;
her careful steps keep ahead of my impetuous racing.
I call out to her:
"Lady, for the sake of the one who loves you,
I beg of you, stop."
She comes to a halt and I can approach.
She says, "It would have been better if you had done
*   that first."*
I remember, and call to her in love,
and wait for her to stop for me.

Soma

May he who, pressed out, is life, is power,
May he whose roaring calls us to the ritual, to drink,
May he, granting gifts, filling us with immortality,
May he, king Soma, be praised in this prayer.
May he, hearing me, come to join me in this rite.
May my words draw him hither.

Thor

Wielder of Mjølnir, Mighty Protector,
Enemy of the Midgard Serpent;
Killer of Giants, Crusher of Foes,
Strider across valleys and mountains:
Thor I praise, friend of people,
and call him to my feast.

Forest Spirits

Within the tangle of bushes and vines,
among the stones and under fallen trees,
the spirits of the forest are waiting for me.
I go to them with gifts as a token of friendship.

☽ ○ ☾

Hidden from me in the forest around me
within each tree, behind each rock,
the spirits of the wild are gathered,
unseen by people who walk, heavy-footed, through
    their world.
I will sit quietly and wait for you,
leaving you these gifts.

The Land Spirits

Surrounded by the forest's trees, I am surrounded by
    the spirits of the forest. I sit here, on the needles
    and leaves, and spread my arms in greeting.
    Come to me, if you wish; I hope for your
    coming. I wait here for you, hoping to see you.
    And if you do not come, I will still leave these
    gifts for you, for my hands are not closed. My

hands are open in generosity toward you, they
are extended in friendship towards you.

☽ ○ ☾

Do you hear me, Land Spirits?
I am calling to you.
Here I am, Land Spirits:
Come to me.
Here are gifts for you:
Come and I will give them.
I am calling you, Land Spirits.
Come and talk to me.

☽ ○ ☾

Riding the sound of the deep drumming
come to me as I call to you.
Come to the rhythm of the heartfelt pounding,
come to me as I call you here.
All of you who inhabit this place
Come to me as I call you here.

[For those who practice shamanism, the drum can be a useful aid for prayer. This particular prayer can be recited over and over, almost like a mantra, until the person praying can feel the numen's presence.]

CHAPTER 7

PRAYERS OF PRAISE

Once you have called the divine beings to you, it is time to praise them. Of course, you don't have to wait for them to come. Praising is good any time.

Prayers of praise also do just what the name implies: they praise the divine being. Prayers of praise can serve as callings as well. Praise forms an image in the mind of the worshipper through which contact can easily be made, and sends out a clear signal to the gods that their presence is desired.

The purpose of prayers of praise is threefold. First, as I have said, they can serve to call a deity to us. Second, they can serve to make us more aware of a deity's presence. The difference here is one of perspective: in the first case, the deity is thought of as not being present, and in the second the deity is already there. That is to say, in the first case, it is the deity who must be reminded and, in the second, it is the worshipper. The third reason for prayers of praise is that the gods deserve them. It is one of the characteristics of divinity that deities are worthy of praise. It is only fitting that we should offer it. No one who has ever had first-hand experience of a deity will have any trouble understanding what I mean.

The appropriateness of prayers of praise may vary with the deity. For instance, when I am in the presence of Cernunnos, I find that my reaction is one of silent awe, rather than of prayer. Nonetheless, I frequently say prayers of praise to him when I wish his presence, falling silent when that is achieved. With Brighid, on the other hand, I find it easy to speak; in fact, speaking to her is the easiest way to ensure her presence. Experience and study will teach you what is appropriate for each deity.

Prayers of praise customarily take two forms, both of which may be combined in one prayer. First, they may consist of titles and descriptions strung together. These are particularly difficult to write, because they tend to degenerate into laundry lists. At their best, however, they can lead to ecstasy—for instance, when the person praying is so attached to the deity that the joy of contact comes with each title and accumulates. A list can be carefully constructed so that each title builds on the preceding one, raising awareness a step higher as each name is spoken.

Prayers of praise can also relate the deeds of a deity. I have already mentioned the Homeric Hymns. What we know of the early stories of the Hindu gods comes from the hymns of the Rig Veda. This technique is similar to the listing of titles, which are often simply short references to myths. I have already mentioned Indra, who slew Vrtra with his vajra, and Thor as "Fenrir's Bane." Myths can also be more clearly related.

> *I praise every god in my daily prayers,*
> *leaving not a single one out.*

The universe does not exclude any of them, so how
   can I?
Praise, praise, to the infinite number of Blessed Ones.
Praise, praise, let there be praise of them all.

[This makes a good prayer for the beginning or the end of the day.]

From all directions about me, the spirits are praying.
The spirits of east and south are praying.
The spirits of west and north are praying.
The spirits of below and above are praying.
The spirits are praying with me.
We all together are praying to the ancient ones.

☽ ○ ☾

Looking out at my yard, I see a leaf falling from a
   tree
and I raise a prayer of awe for the gods
who caused such a marvel to be.

☽ ○ ☾

How shall I find words that can capture the truth?
I am far too bold even to try.
For how many before me have dared this, to praise
   you,
searching themselves for new ways of speaking?
If I could find only one phrase that expressed a
   sunset,
or a word for birds' wings, or a sound for clouds,
I would be content.
But so many are your wonders and so inadequate my
   small attempts

that I can only hope to have reflected some of what
you are.
Or perhaps I serve you best when I fall silent in your
presence.

☽ ○ ☾

What is done in the night,
you see it.
What is done in the day,
you see it.
Who can hide from you,
who are found in all things?
Where would we hide from you,
who are found in all things?
Why would we hide from you,
whose love pours out on all things?

☽ ○ ☾

I think now of the ancient times, when your worship
first was established. It has been a long time
now since your worship was celebrated as it
should be, with processions in the marketplaces,
with games to unite the scattered tribes, with
hospitality granted to strangers in your name.
Throughout the lonely times, you have waited
patiently, in the sure foreknowledge that the
night would end. See now, on the horizon; the
light of dawn begins to creep over the edge of the
world! We need not wait much longer before the
Sun will rise again and shine down once more
on a world in which your worship is no longer
neglected.

Through the long night, we have kept your faith;
in secret or in disguise we have performed the
sacred acts. Sometimes, even unbeknownst to us,
we have kept ancient lore alive. Now we hope to
return to the light, to practice your ways openly
and without fear, drawing the thoughts of others
to you. In the backs of our people's minds, they
have remembered you too.

☽ ○ ☾

Holy Ones of old, we pray to you!
We who have been faithful, pray to you!
Repository of all wisdom,
out of which all others have only a share:
it is to you we look when in need of advice.
The words you speak drop like late summer rains,
refreshing after a drought,
awakening the dormant grass.
Again and again I call to you,
again and again you answer me.
Old and Wise Ones, it is you whom I worship.

☽ ○ ☾

This drink pours out, even as your bounty pours out.
What I do here is only an image of your greater
generosity.

☽ ○ ☾

I pour out libations to the ancient High Ones,
I make my offerings to those who should be
worshipped.

The God

God of the In-between,
you I praise,
you who sit at ease in the midst of chaos,
you who sit at ease on the edge of a sword.
Can anyone attain the mastery you show
as you hold your place between life and death?
Can anyone rival the poise your presence radiates
as you sit in the gateway between past and future?
Can anyone sit so still, but be ready to move
at the exact time the moment requires?
Lord who holds death and life equally in your hands,
I stand in your presence today and give you my
    praise.

☽ ○ ☾

You are a bull, and greatly to be praised,
worthy of sacrifice, Lord of life and death.
You are a ram, and greatly to be praised,
worthy of sacrifice, Lord of life and death.
You are a stallion, and greatly to be praised,
worthy of sacrifice, Lord of life and death.
You are a boar, and greatly to be praised,
worthy of sacrifice, Lord of life and death.
You who are the sacrifice,
You who are the sacrificer,
You who are the Lord of life and death:
Worthy are you, greatly to be praised.[1]

☽ ○ ☾

He is a bull in the field of the gods,
ruling the herd:
worthy of worship, worthy of praise.
He is a stag in the forest of the spirits,
ruling the wilds:
worthy of worship, worthy of praise.
He is a king in the city of the Ancestors,
ruling the world:
worthy of worship, worthy of praise.
The Lord of forests is the Lord of the city,
king of gods, spirits, and Ancestors,
king of people in this world and the next:
worthy of worship, worthy of praise.

[This prayer can also be used as a litany.]

$$\mathbb{D} \; O \; \mathbb{C}$$

You are the hunter.
You are the hunted.
You are the killer.
You are the killed.
Forever going away,
forever coming back,
completing the circle
of life and death.

[This prayer can also be used as a litany.]

$$\mathbb{D} \; O \; \mathbb{C}$$

Wonder and awe, as I sit in your presence,
you who sit in the gateway,
in this world and in the other,
mediating the power that shines through,

letting pass what I need, and what I can use,
holding back in mercy what I cannot.
Seen against the brightness, your dark silhouette
is still and sharp and clear.
Sitting fiercely, with perfect intent,
pure in your purpose, source of terror and comfort.

☽ ○ ☾

A roaring fire, you sit in my heart's center.
A rampaging bull, you tear through my soul.
A searing bolt, you cut through my life.
A skirring arrow, you slice me in two.
A standing stone, you are my anchor.

☽ ○ ☾

A tall-standing oak is our God,
supporting the worlds on his limbs,
each world ordered according to the spreading of his
    branches.
Into each world, his twigs extend,
bearing the leaves and acorns that are our lives.
From what source is this tree nourished?
Where do its roots extend?
Deep within the void they reach
and are fed there from the substance of the Goddess.
He makes known her will, giving it form,
from which we might know it and live according to
    its pattern.
Shaper and essence, open my eyes, open my ears,
    open my heart,
that I might perceive the sacred pattern and conform
    my life to it.[2]

The Goddess

She is the one who is Lady of all,
and she is the one of whom I would speak,
the one who gives birth and the one who brings death,
beginning and end of the course of our lives.

☽ ○ ☾

You are the cauldron of wisdom,
from which inspiration flows.
You are the broad Earth,
which gives birth to all life.
You are the circling Moon,
ruling the tides of oceans and women.
You are the endless night sky,
filled with numberless stars.
You are a grove of birch trees,
shining in the forest deeps.
You are the Mother of us all,
and we look to you in wonder and awe.

☽ ○ ☾

In the dark night sky,
the stars are shining
jewels on the body
of the goddess of night.

☽ ○ ☾

She walked the path that descends to death;
herself still living, she braved the journey
and brought rebirth to those beyond hope
dwelling in the coldest regions,

living in the halls of Earth.
Facing Death boldly, she led him to love
and taught him the secrets that only she knew.
It was her great courage that taught us to dare
and her example that we should follow
in the heart of trouble that may beset us.[3]

☽ ○ ☾

I speak of she who is beyond comparison,
the greatest of mothers
who gave birth to all wonders.
To us, you are Mother,
and to everything else.
The Mother of friends and the Mother of foes.
you do not distinguish between your children,
but spread your love freely
without judgment or preference.

☽ ○ ☾

Here in the center of the turmoil of the city,
I turn my thoughts to her.
Beneath the buildings, deep beneath them,
lies the Earth that is our Mother,
the very body of the Goddess.
She cannot be hidden;
wherever life is found, there she is.
Great Lady, keep me mindful of you
as I walk through the city.

☽ ○ ☾

I raise my voice in praise of the Goddess,
remembering the great things she has done:

they are worth reciting.
She is the one from whose fertile womb everything
we see was born.
They came out from her, ready to be ordered.
Not only in the old time did she do this wonder,
though:
every day is born from between those miraculous
thighs.
Each moment, each event, is continually born from her.
Is this not a miracle?
Is this not worthy of praise?
As continually as you give rise to the world,
just as continually will I praise you.

☽ ○ ☾

Space was born from you in the time before time,
and time itself, and death.
The Dying One was born,
leaping fully armed from your womb,
rising up to order the world.
The waters poured out, to be placed in their proper
locations,
and solid ground was born, to support their weight,
to be the cup of their encircling border.
The directions were placed, each where it belonged.
And life itself was born, the unpredictable,
always yet going where it belongs.
Last of all, and most unpredictable,
your youngest children, we were born,
not always knowing where we belong.
And now I wish to praise the Mother,
who made these things to be,
the source of existence, granter of life.

You to whom we all belong,
you who knows the way we should go,
I praise you with my words,
I hold you in my heart.

☽ ○ ☾

She it is who puts the prayers in my mouth,
and she to whom I speak them.
They come from her, arise in me,
and return again to her,
so that my praying is a part of her eternal cycle;
and when I pray, I take the part she has laid out for
     me.
When I pray, it is her words I pray;
when I sing, it is her song;
when I act, it is her deeds I do.
I cannot step outside the way she has laid out,
for there is nowhere outside to step.
Ground of being, you contain all within you,
both that which acts and that which is acted upon.
Nowhere is there anything that does not arise in you.
Nothing is there that does not praise you by its
     existence.

☽ ○ ☾

I send out words in praise of the Goddess,
from whom all worlds flow.
Mystery of mysteries, this continual creation,
like a fountain forever bubbling up from the Earth's
     darkness,
she is a cup that is never empty.
Generous One, eternally giving gifts,

I pray to you, I praise you,
I remember you throughout my day.

☽ ○ ☾

Goddess of growing things,
of warm and moist earth,
of soil-piercing shoots:
praised in all lands,
praised through all ages,
praised by all peoples,
praised with rites of life.
Mother of All Tribes,
of men and women both,
of beasts and plants and people:
praised in all lands,
praised through all ages,
praised by all peoples,
praised with rites of life.
Queen of all countries,
of crafts and industry,
of poets and of priests:
praised in all lands,
praised through all ages,
praised by all peoples,
praised with rites of life.

[This prayer may be used in a group as a litany, with one person saying the "verses" and the others responding with the "choruses."]

☽ ○ ☾

A lioness protecting her young,
you rage when aroused.
Nothing stands before you,
no troubles can resist you,
no enemies defeat you.
A roaring in the distance announces your arrival,
scattering the dealers of cares.
You shake the Earth beneath their feet,
upsetting all their plans.

[This may be used as a preface to a prayer asking for deliverance from troubles.]

$$\text{☽ ◯ ☾}$$

Wheat for you, Mother of Grain.
Barley for you, Mother of Grain.
Corn for you, Mother of Grain.
I scatter them for you, Mother of Grain:
a tribute to your well-famed generosity.

The Deities

All gods,
all goddesses,
all who are worthy of worship:
hear me.
I remember you in the pouring of this wine.

Apollo

I pray to the one whose arrows bring health and
*   illness,*
to Apollo the beautiful one.

From your lyre come tunes of harmonious
      enchantment,
and I listen enraptured,
sweet-singing Apollo.

Isis

She is the one who sits in protection over the world,
who spreads her wings over us as a shield:
Queen Isis, you are the one I praise!
She is the one who is the throne of kings,
who establishes governments and maintains them in
      power:
Queen Isis, you are the one I praise!
She is the one who rises from the sea in glory,
who rocks the cradle with her own hand:
Queen Isis, you are the one I praise!
She is the one who does not rest until her work is
      done,
who mourns for the dead, crying at our side:
Queen Isis, you are the one I praise!
She is the one who was Queen of Egypt,
who now extends her rule over all the world:
Queen Isis, you are the one I praise!

[This prayer can also be used as a litany.]

Pele

Your hair, the twisting ropes of lava;
your eyes, its glow;
your body, the island cooled from the volcano's
      seething:

how could I not worship you, Pele,
how could I not see how you deserve praise?

Storm God

Ruling the storm, he comes in the night,
loosing his axe again and again.
The Bull of Storms comes bellowing,
scattering seed over the Earth.
A wild beast is he, spreading fire and water as he
    rampages.
In his wake he will leave fertile ground.[4]

Taranis

Brightest bull, Taranis;
wheel wielder, Taranis;
soil soaker, Taranis;
serpent slayer, Taranis.

The Spirits

You there, in the shadows of the edge of the forest.
You there, in the shadows behind the gray stones.
You there, in the shadows beneath the spread
    branches.
You there, in the shadows, I give you my words.

☽ ○ ☾

The people of Earth bless you,
people of spirit,
coming to you with our strength
to use if you wish.

☽ ○ ☾

Spirits of this place,
I honor you with these gifts.

[This short prayer is designed to be used with an offering.]

☽ ○ ☾

I cast grain on the dirt.
I feed the spirits that live there.
I scatter these offerings around me.
I give to those who live in all directions.

☽ ○ ☾

Here, wild ones,
bread from my home, cooked on my hearth,
my gift to you.

CHAPTER 8

LITANIES AND MANTRAS

Litanies, used by groups, and mantras, usually used by individuals, are oddly similar. After reading through this chapter, think back on what you have read and note how easily one can be turned into the other.

Litanies

Litanies are a type of group prayer. One person calls out something, often a title, and the others present respond. The most common responses are phrases like, "We praise you," "We pray to you," "Bless us." I give responses like these in these litanies, but they are easy enough to make up your own.

It is also pretty easy to make up a litany. Simply research the deity you wish to pray to and learn as much as you can about their attributes. Make a list, and bingo—a litany.

Although litanies are, by definition, group prayers, they can actually be used by individuals. The repetition can build to ecstasy. When I use one, I find myself rocking to the rhythm. My whole body prays.

The Goddess

Mother of all,
we praise you, we praise you.
Earth beneath us,
we praise you, we praise you.
Queen of queens,
we praise you, we praise you.
Love of our Lord,
we praise you, we praise you.
Shining lady,
we praise you, we praise you.
Giver of wisdom,
we praise you, we praise you.
Open-handed one,
we praise you, we praise you.

[This can be used to consecrate a Goddess image, passing it from hand to hand as each person calls out a title.]

☽ ○ ☾

Shield of the people,
we honor you, we praise you, we worship you.
Divider of time,
we honor you, we praise you, we worship you.
Well of inspiration,
we honor you, we praise you, we worship you.
Mother of nations,
we honor you, we praise you, we worship you.
Granter of prophecy,
we honor you, we praise you, we worship you.
Seeker of lore,
we honor you, we praise you, we worship you.
Bestower of sovereignty,

we honor you, we praise you, we worship you.
Knower of secrets,
we honor you, we praise you, we worship you.
Encompasser of worlds,
we honor you, we praise you, we worship you.
Mystery of mysteries,
we honor you, we praise you, we worship you.
You who are worthy of honor,
we honor you, we praise you, we worship you.
You who are worthy of praise,
we honor you, we praise you, we worship you.
You who are worthy of worship,
we honor you, we praise you, we worship you.
You who are worthy of honor, praise, and worship,
we honor you, we praise you, we worship you.
You who are worthy of honor, worthy of praise,
      worthy of worship,
we honor you, we praise you, we worship you.

☽ ○ ☾

Earth's Queen
blessings to you, bless us.
Ocean mother
blessings to you, bless us.
Star's breath
blessings to you, bless us.
Heart's rest
blessings to you, bless us.
Life's lover
blessings to you, bless us.
Strong teacher
blessings to you, bless us
First wife

blessings to you, bless us
Love's source
blessings to you, bless us.

Litany for the Animals

Birds of the air,
blessings to you.
Fish of the sea,
blessings to you.
Snakes in your holes,
blessings to you.
Deer in the forest,
blessings to you.
Cattle in the fields,
blessings to you.
[etc.]

Mantras

Andraste

Run before me into battle,
Andraste, protect me in my fight.

Athena

Shaft of reason, light within me.
Clear sight and reason,
open my eyes.

Ba'al

> Ba'al, ride the storm with me.

Brighid

> The fire of Brighid is the flame on my hearth.
> The fire of Brighid is the flame in my heart.

Cernunnos

> Cernunnos, Lord, guide my way.

> Open the way,
> open the way,
> Cernunnos, Lord,
> open the way.

> Disputer of passings, opener of gates,
> Cernunnos, Lord, guide me through.

Gaṇeśa (Gaṇapati)

> Open the way, Gaṇapati.

Gatekeeper deity, such as Cernunnos or Janus

> Watcher on the threshold, guide and guard me.

God of War

> Force and fire, strength of arms.

Gwydion

With magic's might, may Gwydion come.

Inanna

May I descend with Inanna, may I rise with Inanna.

Isis

Isis whose wings support all beings,
be my help, be my supporter.

I call on you Mother, Isis, Queen.

Jupiter

Jupiter, Best and Greatest,
Rule in splendor.

Love Goddess

Love's dear patron, beauty's queen.

Lugh

Bright shield, bright spear, bright Lugh, come.

Ma'at

May no act of mine disturb your feather.

Manannán mac Lir

Over the deeply sounding sea
carry me safely, son of Lir.
Part the mists and guide me through.

Marduk

End the chaos, mighty Marduk.

Mars

Protect my people, ruddy Mars,
with sword upraised be at my side.

Mithra

Thousand-eyed Mithra, may I be just.

Mitra

Lord of oaths, Mitra, friend,
keep my feet clearly on the path of the right.

Mother Goddess

Queen of heaven, bless my home.

Odin

Mead thief and rune snatcher,
with wisdom endow me.

Pan

Awaken me, Pan, walker on the edge,
Lord of mad music, god of wild longings.

Perkunas

My shield and protector, Perkunas, be.

Quetzacoatl

Quetzacoatl, rescue me.

Rhiannon

Great Queen Rhiannon, guide and protect me.

My guide is Rhiannon as I ride through life.

River Goddess

Life's soft fluid, gently welling,
source and gift to all who live.

Taranis

Taranis, Thunderer, be my protector.

Defeat my foes with flashing flame,
with thunder and lightning, Taranis, lord.

Thor

Smasher of serpents, empower me, Thor.

Thoth

I ask to write truth on the tablet of life.

Venus

Venus of beauty, grant my desire.

CHAPTER 9

THANKSGIVING PRAYERS AND GRACES

The gods give us much. The entire world may be seen as a gift from them. They keep it running, and this should be acknowledged. It is only fair to thank them for it. It behooves us to be at least as polite to the gods as we are to each other. By making such prayers regularly, you are also reminded of your place in the cosmic order.

Thanks can be given for individual blessings or for general ones. If you pray to Asklepios for healing and you are healed, thank him. Don't let the fact that the doctor gave you antibiotics serve as an excuse for not doing so. You prayed, you owe, and who is to say that Asklepios has not worked through the medium of the doctor or drugs?

A related sort of prayer is the payment of a vow. This can be the second half of a two-part prayer: in the first part, you promise to do something—give an offering, usually—if a deity does something for you. Then it's time to pay. A deal's a deal.

Thanksgiving Prayers

Thank you, O mighty ones,
for all you have done for me.
May I not forget you, though the world turn against me.
Though I fall with my enemies rejoicing about me,
it will be your presence that will comfort me,
and I will still thank you for the incomparable
rightness of every moment.

☽ ○ ☾

The gifts the gods give me are many and wonderful
and I am grateful to the gods for their generosity.
Knowing that it would be wrong to forget them,
I lift my voice in thankfulness.
Holy Ones, thank you, for all that you have done.

☽ ○ ☾

Standing in the presence of the mighty gods,
my mind is turned toward all I've been given.
I thank them, as is only their due,
for they pour out blessings on all their children.

☽ ○ ☾

It is only fair to thank you, blessed ones:
You have given me so much;
I give to you from my little.

☽ ○ ☾

Sitting in the presence of those who deserve praise,
I turn my thoughts to thankfulness,
thinking of the gifts they have granted to the world
they love so well.
Intertwined with the world's substance,
the gods have created and sustained,
brought forth and upheld,
wonders beyond humanity's lifetimes' imagining.
Out of the multitude of scattered gifts,
I have been witness to only a few.
Yet still I experience awe;
still I am moved to gratitude;
still I approach you with thanks.
Givers of gifts, accept my words as my own gift to
you in return.

☽ ○ ☾

From you have come answers to my prayer.
From me come offerings in gratitude.
See what I give you:
a grateful offering with grateful words.

☽ ○ ☾

In payment of my vow, I offer [offering] to [name of
god or spirit].

[It doesn't get much simpler than this.]

☽ ○ ☾

Open hands deserve open hands.

[This is something you can tack onto a calling or prayer of praise to
turn it into a thanksgiving. It goes with an offering, of course.]

Thanks to my patron for my continued prosperity,
for my continued health, for my continued life.
Continually I will pray to you,
always remembering you.

☽ ○ ☾

From you have flowed freely many gifts,
given with no conditions, offered with open hands.
Continually you have renewed the world with your
     largesse;
Continually you have brought new wonders into
     being.
I come before you, then, with unnecessary gratitude;
no matter what my actions are, yours will not
     change.
What you do is in perfect accord with your nature.
I wish to be more like you, to take you as my model,
And, though my gifts may be unnecessary for you,
they are all too vital for me.
I hold them out to you, then, generous ones.
See—I am generous too.

☽ ○ ☾

The circle turns, it turns around,
carrying me with it, and I turn too.
These wonderful things that came from the gods
are being returned to them, to keep the turning going.

☽ ○ ☾

The balance is kept:
I do not only take,
I also know how to give.

The Goddess

The Goddess has given birth to another wonder
in this marvelous life of mine.
I will thank her daily for the gift of life
and for all she distributes from her free and open hands.

☽ ○ ☾

I am burning incense to the Queen of Heaven,
a sweet smell on Earth to bring her to mind,
to give her the best of what I have,
as is only her proper share.

Ocean Spirits

A perfect feather I found on the beach
I place on the sea's edge for the waves to take,
a gift for the ocean spirits,
completing the circle.

Wind Spirits

The spirits are riding on the wind.
Here is a gift for you:
flour, the raw stuff of food,
scattered in the air to be carried away with you.

Graces

Prayers over food and drink are a special type of thanksgiving prayer. The connection between them is shown quite strongly in the North American harvest festivals that have been given the name "Thanksgiving."

As Pagans, we believe that it is not only the gods we should thank for our food, but the food itself. Our eating is a constant reminder of one of the central mysteries of neo-Paganism, the connection between life and death. Our life depends on the death of our food, so it is only proper that we should thank that food.

Eating is, in fact, a sacrifice. In ancient times, this was made clear, because sacrificed animals were eaten. People think of sacrifices as being about giving up, when actually they are about sharing. People shared their animals with the gods and with each other. Eating together draws people together, and eating with the gods brings us closer to them.

Even though we no longer conduct religious sacrifices, we take part in the give-and-take of life and death. Even today, we can think of the killing required for food (even vegetables die to feed us) as a kind of sacrifice, to be acknowledged to the deities, and to the animal and plant spirits.

Consider that you might want to do this in reverse. Instead of a sacrifice being your food, let your food be a sacrifice. The Romans gave a bit of their food at each meal to the hearth goddess. It would not be a bad idea to offer a bit of yours to her, or to the Ancestors, or to your family's patrons—if not at every meal, then at least regularly.

> *I am setting a place at my table for the High Gods.*
> *Blessed ones, come and eat with me!*
> *I am setting a place at my table for the gods of my*
>   *household.*
> *Blessed ones, come and eat with me!*
> *I am setting a place at my table for the Ancestors.*

Blessed ones, come and eat with me!
I am setting a place at my table for the Land Spirits.
Blessed ones, come and eat with me!
Numinous ones of Earth and Sky,
eat with me, be my guests.

☽ ○ ☾

I invite the Holy Ones to my table.
Come; sit with me, eat and drink with me.
I offer you the hospitality of my home.
You are always welcome here.

☽ ○ ☾

We sit down to the table of the gods
where the company of heaven meet,
and we share with them our food.
Blessed ones, be our dining companions!

☽ ○ ☾

Upon this food, place your blessings, Holy Ones.
Our eating of it is a ritual of praise for all you have
*   done.*

☽ ○ ☾

Come, holy gods, and bless this food that will feed
my body, through the actions of which you are
daily made manifest in the world.

☽ ○ ☾

This food is the work of many made palpable.
Before eating, it is right to acknowledge their labor.
We thank all of these people
and all their protective spirits.

☽ ○ ☾

In the sacrificial fire, I place an offering of food:
I send my prayers to the god with my body.
Holy Ones, receive this offering.
Be honored by it, by my life's true sacrifice.
The food that I eat is offered to you.

[Here, the sacrificial fire is the life within us. We place our food on it, and bless the gods with whom we have relationships.]

☽ ○ ☾

I pour out this drink to you, Holy One:
share my good fortune.
I place this food out for you, Holy One:
share my friendship.

☽ ○ ☾

How wonderful!
How marvelous!
This food is the gift of the Earth from which it grew.

☽ ○ ☾

How wonderful!
How marvelous!
This food is the gift of those who drew it forth and
Those who prepared it.
How wonderful!

How marvelous!
This food is the gift of the gods and goddesses.
How wonderful!
How marvelous!
We give, in return, our thoughts and prayers,
our words and deeds.
A gift for a gift,
with thanks to the givers.
How wonderful!
How marvelous!

The God and Goddess

Models for our lives,
Lady and Lord,
when we eat this food, we are doing as you do,
taking part in the chain of life and death.
Bless this food, then,
that it might nourish both body and spirit.

Food Spirits

Plants whose lives I take,
animals whose deaths I cause:
here you are remembered,
and your endings are not for nothing.
I tell you this:
your deaths will be transformed into life
and that life will be one of which the gods will approve,
one lived in honor of their sacred law.

Come, spirits of my food,
and feed my life.
We will live our lives together from now on,
you living in me.

Prayer for Alcohol

Dionysos

Within this water lurks fire
and so it is a dangerous thing,
where opposites dwell in balance.
But the dangerous spots of in-between
are also the places of power.
God of ecstasy, guide us in the proper use
of this thing of danger and power.
May we use it well for your purposes.

CHAPTER 10

PRAYERS FOR TIMES OF THE DAY

By praying at the special times of the day, Pagans put themselves in accord with the daily pattern of time. This assures that, in other ways, they will act in accord with nature. Just as important, it is only right to begin and end the day with thoughts of the gods. They deserve it.

> *As comings in and goings out,*
> *my prayers bracket my day.*

Since, in most neo-Pagan traditions, the Sun is male and a symbol of the God, I have addressed most of these solar prayers to a god. In the ancient Pagan religions, however, the Sun was frequently female, and the dawn as well, as shown by the Greek Eos, the Hindu Usas, the Roman Aurora, and the Germanic Eostre, all of whose names are related and mean "Rising."

Prayers at Dawn

The God

From Mother Night, the God is born,
returning to us, pouring out blessings.
I raise my hands to the new-born babe
Who, even so young, does not hesitate,
but rides forth manfully in his shining wheeled
*   chariot.*
Rise up on the right path, Lord;
rise up and distribute your light freely
as a king in his hall scatters gold

Dawn

Scatter your welcome light, Dawn,
as freely as a hostess spreading a feast for guests.
Place before us the banquet of this day's deeds
and we will share it with you.

Eos

The goddess of dawn sends her maidens before her
as heralds to announce the coming of the light.
There, in the east, the light increases and she
*   appears on the horizon.*
Eos, bring the dawn.
Eos, bring the light.
Eos, bring the day.

The Sun

I set my face toward the eastern horizon
and wait, in the dark, for the coming of day.
See, there, he rises, the shining one rises,
and I stand here praising, revering the wonder.

☽ ○ ☾

On the rim of the world, she is dancing.
In her bright robe, she is dancing.
Young and lovely, she is dancing.
Bringer of vision, she is dancing.
Dance, Sun maiden, into the sky,
bringing the day to those who wait for you.

☽ ○ ☾

As the Sun rises, I face his glory,
grateful that the darkness has come to an end.
Though darkness is sacred, its soothing a gift,
I am a human, a creature of light.
So I face you in thankfulness
and greet your return with praises and prayer
and the honor that is due you.

☽ ○ ☾

I raise my hands in honor to the Lord of the morning,
who rises in glory in the east of the world.
Piercer of darkness, illumine my path as I go
     through my day.
Way-shower, illumine my path as I go through my life.

☽ ○ ☾

Rise up, rise up, Sun in the east,
while the world turns toward you.
It has turned toward you since its very beginning,
in infinite longing, in infinite love.
And I, a child of Earth, take her as my exemplar,
and hold my heart out to you in the dawn.

☽ ○ ☾

You have returned, O Sun, as I knew you would,
for this is your part in the way of things.
You have your role, and you play it well.
I ask that you inspire me to do the same:
to know the right thing to do
and to do it with passion and joy and honor.

☽ ○ ☾

Praises to you, Sun in the east;
as you are born from the womb of night,
I praise you.

☽ ○ ☾

Leap up, leap up,
young god, young warrior,
rise into the sky as into a battle,
dispelling the darkness that has covered the world,
putting to flight the fears of the night.

☽ ○ ☾

She has given birth to you again;
again you climb the sky,
again you reach for your glory,

again I stand here to praise you.[1]
The sacred path is fulfilled,
things are as they should be.
Rising Sun, herald of the right way,
I praise you!

☽ ○ ☾

A rooster heralding the dawn,
I crow my praise to the Sun that rises.
Amazing! Wonderful!
Every morning, again and again:
Amazing! Wonderful!

☽ ○ ☾

Hail to you, Sun, rising in the east,
scattering before you the terrors of the night
as a cat among pigeons.
No mere cat are you, though:
a young lion, roaring into the sky,
blazing eagerly into the tasks of the day.
Enflame me, young lord;
suit me for the tasks ahead.

☽ ○ ☾

As a queen comes into her own,
entering her throne room,
smiling on all who wait there;
just like that, shining lady,
rise.

☽ ○ ☾

You give birth to yourself, Mother Sun.
Each day this great Mystery.

☽ ○ ☾

Again the boat sails, carrying the Sun.
Again the wagon rolls, carrying the Sun.
Carry it well and true in its well-worn path.[2]

Uṣas and Sūrya

The Earth rolls forward with silent thunder,
turning toward the Sun in the false dawn.
I stand on the wet grass, anticipating the sunrise.
While, far away, at the edge of vision,
the goddess Dawn opens her gates and the Sun
enters the day.
Open your gates wide, youthful one, do not hold
*   back.*
Open your gates, Uṣas, and let Surya stride forth,
so the morning prayers might start
and the day's business begin.

Prayers for the Morning

It is my privilege to perform my morning prayers.
It is my honor to do what should be done.
As I rise with the morning, fog lifting slowly from my
*   mind,*
I pray not to forget these truths.

The Goddess and the God

Mother of All, Father of All:
as I go through the day,
keep my eyes open wide.
May I not miss beauty.
May I not miss joy
May I not miss wonder.
Keep me awake and aware of the world.

All the Gods

In the morning, everything is new.
The day's blank slate lies before me,
ready for my writing.
May it be words of beauty I write.
May it be deeds of grace I do.
May it be thoughts of joy I think.
All the Holy Ones, listen:
this is what I pray.

☽ ○ ☾

My day begins again,
and again I dedicate myself to the service of the gods.
May it be their tasks I perform.

The Sun

As the day wears on, keep before my eyes, Shower of
*   the Way,*
the path of the Holy Ones,
that I may not forget that it is to them that I have
*   dedicated my life,*
so that every action may be an offering to them.

☽ ○ ☾

The tears of the dawn still sparkle on the grass as I
begin my day.
God of beginnings, bless my beginning.
Open paths before me, make easy the way.
May I go through the day with ease
and end it in thankfulness.

☽ ○ ☾

Bright youth, newly born, I pray to you.
A fresh day has been given to me;
may I be worthy of the gift.

☽ ○ ☾

I stand in the morning
and face the east
and greet the Sun
and a new day.

The Ancestors

Your blood is my blood,
flowing out of the past, through me, to the future.
Through my actions, you live.
Guide me, then, in the decisions I face today,
making clear to me the safe path between obstacles
and keeping me from false steps along the way.

[With "today" in the fourth line changed to "each day," this may also
be used as a New Year's prayer.]

Prayer for a Lie-Abed

I am here to pray long hours after the Sun has risen.
While the day began, I was still asleep, still walking
in the land of dreams.
Know this, bright Sun, that though I slept, you were
still in my heart.
Now, when I am finally awake, I take up my daily
responsibilities.
First, though, I will stand here and drink in your
warmth
and drink in all the light you give so freely
to arm myself for the day's struggles.

Prayers for the Noontime

From high above, the Sun looks down,
the witness of all deeds done by the people.
Lord of Truth, guide me in my actions,
so that all that I do might be worthy of your gaze.

☽ ○ ☾

You have mounted to your throne in the roof
of heaven,
you have achieved the heights.
In the midpoint of the day, you rule
from the midpoint of the sky.
Lord of Light, I praise you as you shine!

☽ ○ ☾

The great shining eye that sees all things
will see that my deeds are done justly.
I place myself under your gaze
at the high point of the day.

☽ ○ ☾

Praise to the Sun, at the roof of the world.
Praise to him, at his point of great power.

☽ ○ ☾

Look up, look up, at the glorious Sun,
the world calls to me, and says "Look up!"
From high above, I can feel the heat descending,
warming me as I walk here below.
I wish to look up, but my eyes are not meant for such
    power.
I will feel the warmth, though,
and thank you, Lord Sun.

☽ ○ ☾

Though you are high above, your heat still reaches
    me,
testing my endurance as I work under its glare.
Do not give me more testing than I can handle,
and do not insult me by giving me less.

☽ ○ ☾

Following your course, laid down in ancient times,
you have come unerringly to the heights of the sky,
there where you can survey the wide Earth with no
    obstruction.

May all on which you gaze be to your liking!
May all below follow its course as well as you!

☽ ○ ☾

Hail to you, noontide Sun, high in the southern sky.
A king in full power are you,
sitting high in the heavens' throne room.
And I come to you, as a faithful subject,
to ask you to stretch forth your many shining hands
and lay them on my head in benediction.

☽ ○ ☾

Your blossom fully open, shining.
Your bloom in full beauty, shining.
Your face in full radiance, shining.
See me from on high, Bright Queen,
watch over me, shining.

Prayers for Afternoon

Prayer for the Workday's End

With the day over, let me rest, Holy Ones.
I have earned this quiet time by my day's labors.
Come and share my ease, come and rest with me.
Surround me and support me,
be my rest, my peace, my home.

Prayer for Rush Hour

You who guide travelers,
slide me through traffic.
You who grant patience,
help me wait calmly.

Prayers for Sunset

The ship reaches its haven.
The wagon reaches its home.
Today's journey is over and all can rest.
Those who have guided the Sun in its journey:
Thank you.
May you guide me as well.

Night

Great blackness, promiser of mysteries, bringer of
dreams:
greetings to you, Mother Night, as you cast your
blanket over the world!

Sun

At the close of day, I face the west,
the direction of rest,
and raise my hands in prayer to the Sun.
Great shining one, may I go to my rest with your
*   regards*
as you go to yours with mine.

☽ ○ ☾

As you lower yourself through the sky toward the
    horizon,
I hold your red disk between my hands.
You who fill my hands, fill my heart
and stay with me through the dark time,
until morning comes again

☽ ○ ☾

The eagle ends his flight
and goes to his well-earned sleep in his western
    aerie.
So too will I go to mine when the time is right,
that I might rise again tomorrow and take flight with
    him.

☽ ○ ☾

Hail to you, Sun setting in the west.
As you close your day, you end your long journey.
As for me, I too will soon begin my time of rest.
But first, I will one more time face you as you sit on
    the horizon
and once more raise my hands in praise.

☽ ○ ☾

Lord of the West, enthroned on the world's edge,
I pray to you at the end of the day,
offering to you my day's actions
on the altar of the fiery sky.
Accept them; take them to yourself,
purifying me of my errors,
blessing me in my good deeds.

Darkness descends, as the Sun lowers itself behind
the horizon
and I stand facing the last light, with my shadow at
my back.
Farewell to you, Lord of Light, as you go to your
rest.
I turn to face the darkness and greet it without fear.

[At the line, "I turn to face," do just that; face the east. Once it held the
morning, and now it brings the dark.]

I bow to the setting Sun,
lowering myself as it descends over the world's edge.

Our burning queen lowers herself to bed
to rest for tomorrow's travel.
I, too, will soon go to my bed,
resting with the dreams the Holy Ones send.

Spirits of Day and Night

As around our home the darkness grows,
I light the evening lights.
As the daytime spirits depart, I say my goodbyes:
you will stay in our hearts the whole night through.
As the nighttime spirits gather about, I give greetings
*   to them:*
may these lights honor you who come with the
darkness.

Prayers for Bedtime

As I go to bed, I pray to the High Gods.
I offer you my worship, and ask you to bless my family.
I ask if I have done anything today to offend you.
If I have, I ask for forgiveness and for guidance,
that I might walk the sacred path in peace and in
     beauty.
As I go to bed, I pray to the gods of my household.
I offer you my worship and ask you to bless my
     family.
I ask if I have done anything today to offend you.
If I have, I ask for forgiveness and for guidance,
that I might walk the sacred path in peace and in
     beauty.
As I go to bed, I pray to the Ancestors.
I do you honor and ask you to bless my family.
I ask if I have done anything today to offend you.
If I have, I ask for forgiveness and for guidance,
that I might walk the sacred path in peace and in
     beauty.
As I go to bed, I pray to the Land Spirits.
I do you honor and ask you to bless my family.
I ask if I have done anything today to offend you.
If I have, I ask for forgiveness and for guidance,
that I might walk the sacred path in peace and in
     beauty.
As I go to bed, I pray to all numinous beings.
I do you honor and ask that you extend your
     blessings over me and mine.

☽ ○ ☾

Before I go to sleep, I extend my thoughts to all in
my house
and ask that we might live together in peace.
Before I go to sleep, I extend my thoughts to the
human community,
and ask that we might live together in peace.
Before I go to sleep, I extend my thoughts to all
living creatures,
and ask that we might live together in peace.
Before I go to sleep, I extend my thoughts to the
Holy Ones,
and ask that we might live together in peace.
Shining ones, whose care extends over the whole
world,
bless the world with peace.

☽ ○ ☾

May the Lord and the Lady protect me as I lie in bed.
May they bring me dreams of pleasure and guidance.
May they wake me in the morning rested and
refreshed.

The God and the Goddess

Sleep, little one, in the comforting night
that spreads like a blanket over your bed.
The Goddess is waiting to guide you to sleep
in her arms that are ready to rock you so gently.
The God stands by, watching to keep you from harm,
to lay his cool hand on your head as you sleep.
Sleep, little one, in the gathering dark,
wrapped in the love of your Mother and Father,
wrapped in the love of your mother and father.

Sleep

Welcoming sleep, I spread my arms in response to
your ever-open ones.
Take me to yourself softly,
as a knitter returns a scattered skein to order,
rolling it into a ball;
even so, draw me in, restore me,
open the door to your world that I might enter.

Prayers for Night

Night is called the first of all things because of the common belief that the world came out of darkness. In part, this reflects the obvious truth that before something there was nothing, and that "nothing" is equated with darkness. The connection between these two is not so subtle, however. For, after all, if light (and everything else) was born out of darkness, how can that darkness be thought of as nothing? It is a creative force in itself. Thus, among the Celts and Germans, the day began with night, and the year with winter. To this day, our day begins in the middle of night and our year in the middle of winter.

The world rests beneath night's blanket
and I sit quietly, finally myself at rest.
All day, I have been the one talking;
my time for silence has arrived.
Speak to me, Holy Ones, and I will listen.
Here I am, waiting to hear your words.

[Nighttime, with its silence, is a good time for allowing the gods to speak.]

Night

I speak of darkness from out of darkness,
of night from out of night.
Night I praise, the first of all things,
the blackness within which worlds are formed.
In the encompassing embrace of the arms of night,
everything was held that has existence.
From under the blanket that she lays over us,
everything came forth that has existence.
Birthplace of all, to you I pray:
Worthy are you to be praised.

☽ ○ ☾

The womb of night will give birth to day
when the proper time has passed.
Though I long for day, in my heart I know
that the way things are is done rightly.
Here in the dark, I remember this
and rest in the sure concern of the Holy Ones.

Spirits of the Darkness

Spirits of the darkness, you are my friends:
though the night's blackness stands as a wall, you
*   will show me the way through,*
my guides through shadows,
my protectors from all terrors.

Prayer for an Insomniac

From the deep emptiness of a sleepless night,
my pleas are sent to the gods of sleep.

To the givers of dreams I call,
to those who come in the night, not as dangers,
but as bringers of peace.
Come to me, as I lie alone in the dark.
Slip quietly through the night and place your hands
    on my brow,
soothing me gently until I slide into sleep.

CHAPTER 11

PRAYERS FOR TIMES OF THE MONTH

Wheels within wheels, cycles within cycles. You will see that the chapters in this book go from shorter periods of time (days) to longer ones (life events). The next is that of the month.

The month was originally defined by Moons; a month was the duration of a Moon. The only month left on our calendar with this length is February, and even that is not connected with the Moon directly. Old calendars were very closely connected to the Moon, however. Because the lunar year and the solar year don't match up, some system was needed to bring the two back into alignment. The most common method was to add a month every few years. The Jewish calendar is a well-known example of this. The modern calendar is solar, so if you are going to follow the patterns of the Moon, you will have to pay special attention to them. Of course, this is good, since Pagans should be paying attention to what is going on in the world around them, rather than relying on an abstract system such as the modern calendar. In this chapter, then, when I speak of months, I mean Moons.

The Moon measures time. In fact, the earliest evidence of counting we have may be records of Moon phases. The word "Moon" actually comes from a root meaning "to measure." The Moon is the measurer, then. It measures out time, and it measures out our lives.

Since most neo-Pagans are Wiccan, the most common attitude toward the Moon is that it is a symbol of the Goddess. This belief has roots deep in our culture, both secular and neo-Pagan, mostly due to the influence of Greek culture. Wicca has also adopted the concept of the Triple Goddess, as expressed by Robert Graves; the Maiden, the Mother, and the Crone. They are connected with the waxing Moon, the Full Moon, and waning Moon, respectively.

Most of the prayers to the Moon given here are written with these two concepts in mind: the Moon is the Goddess, and the Moon's different forms correspond to the different forms of the Goddess. There is, however, also a time of the month when there is no Moon, the time between the waning and waxing Moons. This is usually called the "New Moon," a term I find peculiarly inaccurate. The New Moon, it seems to me, is the first crescent after the dark period. I therefore call the dark period "the Dark Moon," and reserve "New Moon" for the waxing crescent.

This is the not the only way of looking at the Moon found in ancient Paganism. Some saw the Moon as male. In Hinduism, for instance, the Moon is Soma, the god of the inspiring sacred drink. The Man in the Moon comes from a Germanic belief that the Moon is male. I give a prayer, then, to the Proto-Indo-European Ménôts, the masculine Moon, measurer of time.

Prayers for the New Moon

Chase your Father, little one;
swiftly he sinks and swiftly you follow him.
Grow in strength and in sureness.
Grow into yourself as the month goes by.

☽ ○ ☾

Out of the bright sky, as the Sun goes down,
appears the Maiden who rules the darkness.
I pray to her, my eyes facing west
at the end of the day,
at the beginning of the month.
You will not be here with us long;
you dance quickly toward the horizon.
While you are still with us, though,
I will look on you with love.
Hope in the west, prophet of return from darkness:
you show us it is possible to go from age into the
*   shadowland*
and emerge, new yet the same.

☽ ○ ☾

When I am surrounded by the shadows,
come to me and remind me of this night's lesson
I pray to you, who wear the silver crescent,
not to let me forget.

☽ ○ ☾

What is that there, appearing in the purple west,
what swims into sight as the Sun sets?
A new Moon is shining.
You have followed the Sun,
and now you are ready to take your own place.
Welcome, New Moon,
Welcome, Sweet Maiden.

☽ ○ ☾

From out of the brightness, the Maiden appears,
dancer, singer, seducer, scattering flowers.
From out of the darkness, the Maiden appears,
dancer, singer, seducer, scattering flowers.
Pruning sickle, encourage new growth,
dance and sing and seduce
and scatter your flowers over the Earth.[1]

Ménōts

Ménōts who marks the passing of days,
with your sharp edges, cut out this month
from the time before and the time after.
Measure it out to fit the pattern laid out for you.

Prayers for the Full Moon

Queen of Night, your silver wheel rolls silently
through the darkness
from sunset to sunrise on this night when you are full.
I look on you in awe, and praise you.
I look to you in love, and honor you.

Lamp of the night,
guide my way.
Shine from above me,
a light in the darkness.

As the Sun retreats you enter the sky.
Give birth to the night, Great Mother.
Give birth to your children that fill the dark sky.
Give birth to our dreams that will fill our sleep.

Your silver disk will light the entire night;
none of the night will be turned over to the dark.
Even as your soft light guides my path tonight,
may your gentle influence spread softly through my
     life.

Round face of the Mother,
look down on me in blessing;
light my way through darkness.

With such brilliant light, to rival the Sun,
can you be said to move in darkness?
A light for the shadows
a lantern for those abroad,
a guide for travelers:

throughout the night you continue to bless us,
faithful Moon.

$$\text{☽ ○ ☾}$$

I pour out milk to the Queen of Heaven,
the Mother of Wonders, shining tonight.
The pool that it forms mirrors you there
as you look down on me.
Accept this milk as a thank you for all that you give
        so freely.[2]

$$\text{☽ ○ ☾}$$

This small bowl of drink is yours, Lady of the Moon,
its round brightness reflecting your shining wheel.
I place it on the grass, and invite you to come with
        your children to share it.

$$\text{☽ ○ ☾}$$

It is time to be full,
just as it was time to be dark.
With the month duly measured,
with respect for the dark,
I turn to you with joy.

Prayers for the Waning Moon

The Old Woman takes her place
in the early morning
in the dome of the sky.
Though guardian of the darkness,

and though yourself of advanced age,
you are yet the prophet of the Sun,
promising his imminent rebirth.
Old One, Wise One, Crone in the East,
Anna, I look on you with reverence
and praise you in the moments before dawn.

☽ ○ ☾

I ask for wisdom from the Old One,
enlightenment in the late hours of night.

☽ ○ ☾

You gathered light into a ball
and now you unravel it again.
Soon it will be gone and we will face the dark.
But we know it will end in the proper time,
because you are the Lord of Right Measure
and you always do what has been laid down for you.

☽ ○ ☾

The sickle of reaping is low in the sky in the period
just before dawn.
The Sun's halo soon will hide it, but still it will be
there,
at the back of my mind, at the bottom of my heart,
poised to perform its acts of loving mercy.
Waning Moon, pass over me, and pass on by.
Grant me your wisdom, but withhold your power.[3]

Prayers for the Dark Moon

It will be a dark night indeed,
for, even though the stars give what light they can,
it comes from far away, and is scattered and spent
when it falls on the Earth.
Where is the light that comes from nearer,
from our own world's companion, our own world's
    sister?
She hides from us tonight.
Tonight there will be no Moon.
Tonight we will have no companion to guide us
through the darkness.
But though we cannot see you, you live in our hearts.
Strengthen us in the darkness:
is that not what darkness is for?

☽ ○ ☾

This is a night when the Moon is away with her
lover, the Sun,
and we will not see her, though we wait until dawn.
But when dawn does come, she will be there,
and if we do not see her with our eyes,
to our hearts she should be visible.
Dark Lady, open our hearts,
keep them aware of you.

☽ ○ ☾

Mysterious Darkness, I pray to you,
you who transform want into plenty.
Even as, in your hidden realm, the Moon is reborn,
so, too, might hope be reborn in me.

Queen of Darkness, may the night pass soon.
Queen of Darkness, preserve me until light's return.

☽ ○ ☾

With no Moon's light to break the black night,
we wait with patience for change to come.
Pure Moon Goddess, change in me what changes in
*   you.*
Bring me through dark times. Bring me rebirth.

☽ ○ ☾

A night that is dark,
a time of change,
mystery of mysteries.
During my dark hours, dark ones,
may I glimpse the mystery
and see ahead of me the newly rising Moon.

☽ ○ ☾

Dark Queen:
from a time that is dark,
bring back light to my world.

☽ ○ ☾

Darkness is for silence.
This I know, Dark Moon.
Just a few words of remembrance, then,
and I will keep the silence with you.

CHAPTER 12

PRAYERS FOR TIME
OF THE YEAR

Prayers for the times of the year can be especially tricky to write. Many forms of neo-Paganism have a myth of the year, a storyline that runs through all of the seasons, describing the actions of the gods and the goddesses at each point along the way. The dates most commonly celebrated by neo-Pagans are the eight festivals of Wicca: Samhain (Halloween), Yule (Winter Solstice), Imbolc (February 2nd), Ostara (Spring Equinox), Beltane (May Day), Midsummer (Summer Solstice), Lammas (August 1st), and Harvest (Fall Equinox). This composite of Celtic, Germanic, and Christian holy days was devised by Gerald Gardner and his followers in the middle of the twentieth century, but it calls on ancient principles and has struck a chord with many people today.

Problems arise when we try to write prayers that correspond to the meaning of each of these days. Although the different traditions of Wicca agree on the days to be celebrated, they disagree on what is being celebrated. For instance, some Wiccans follow Robert Graves in putting a battle between the waxing and waning years at Midsummer. Others follow the Welsh evidence and place a similar battle at Beltane. Norse customs and legends surrounding Yule are similar to Celtic ones associated with Samhain. Moreover, there is the obvious problem of differing climates. A prayer that is appropriate at May Day in New Hampshire is not going to be appropriate for the same day in Mississippi.

What I have done, then, is to write most of these prayers, not for particular dates in the neo-Pagan calendar, but rather for seasonal events. In that way, they can be applied more easily to different myths of the year and different climates. Some will still be inappropriate to some climates, but they may still serve as examples.

I have also included prayers for secular occasions. Since all is sacred, there really is no such thing as a secular occasion, no event that cannot be observed with prayer. If it is the goal of neo-Paganism to reawaken a sense of the sacred in everyday life, it is only fitting that we should make the secular sacred.

These prayers may be added to your regular daily prayers, either in the morning or at night. They may also be included in group rituals, or said at meal time.

Prayers for the Festival of the Dead

I pray to all the gods of death,
of darkness, of sorrow.
Though I do not love you, I respect you.
Though I do not welcome you, I honor you.

Though I do not invite you into my life,
I know you are already there.

☽ ○ ☾

Eat with us, Ancestors,
on this night of the dead.
Share our meal with us
and then go on your way.

Prayers for Winter

Winter is not just a single day. It takes its time. Pay attention to its different stages, and adjust your prayers accordingly.

Prayers for the Beginning of Winter

As the cold time begins,
I turn toward it with courage,
knowing I do not face it alone.
All the Holy Ones are with me;
we will face it together.

☽ ○ ☾

The leaves may fall,
the grass may die,
but the Land Spirits live,
and to them I pray.
Though some may sleep,
others awake
to face the cold,

to bless the Earth
with the gifts only they can give.
Spirits of rock and tree,
Spirits of running and still water,
Spirits of Earth and sky:
to the ones who now go to sleep,
farewell until the warm time.
To those who now awake,
once again I greet you,
as the Earth once again enters winter.

Prayer for Early Winter

Cry the winter rains to prepare the way,
to mourn the darkness now enfolding.
Cry the winter rains to prepare the way,
to wash pure the world as it lies here waiting.
Cry the winter rains, sky overarching,
but soon the sorrows' tears will turn to joy.
Light will return to the covered Earth.
Cry, rain spirits, as this time demands.

Prayers for Deep Winter

Raised against the empty winter sky, the barren
limbs of trees and my hands reach out in prayer.
I ask from the gods of winter the strength I will need
to endure until spring
and the wisdom I require to learn from the dark and
the cold the lessons they will teach.
May I receive them without flinching.

☽ ○ ☾

With silent steps you come, snow spirits,
silently descending, silently landing.
You who silence the world with your falling,
silence it so I can hear from you:
I hear silence.

☽ ○ ☾

Underneath the thick white blanket,
may the Earth sleep, dreaming,
till, rested and refreshed, it bursts free again.
Goddesses and gods of land and field,
may it be this winter as it has always been.

Prayer for the Rainy Season

Drop welcome tears upon the Earth,
fertile sky.
Awaken it to new life,
feed its thirsty mouth.

Prayers for Yule

This is the long night.
This is the dark night.
This is the cold night.
This is the night of last hope.
This is the night of the little spark.
This is the night of turning from darkness.
This is the night of turning toward light.
This is the night of wonder.

The long night is here:
come to us, you spirits;
together let us fill the long night with light,
calling all beings to warm themselves at our fires.

The Goddess

How is it that you give birth to everything, Lady,
never once growing infertile?
Even in the cold time, when everything seems dead,
each moment is born after its predecessor
and time goes on: you give birth even in the poverty
of winter.

Sun

Around me burn the lights of Yule;
I am filled with their light,
renewed by their light.
I pray to you, new Sun,
Reborn, O Lord, from the dark.

☽ ○ ☾

Happy birthday, Sun!
The whole world is spread beneath you,
wrapped in darkness,
as a present for you to open.

Prayers for the New Year

These prayers are specifically for the beginning of the secular year, for January 1st. They invoke Janus, from whose name the word "January" comes. The second one involves pouring out wine. I do this every year on New Year's Eve, or, if I am away visiting friends, before I enter my house on my return. I pour it out on the threshold, and use some to anoint the door posts. The lid on the inside of the threshold that makes for a tight seal also prevents the wine from flowing into the house. The red stain on my doorstep, which lasts for a while, may confuse the neighbors, but while it is there, it is a reminder to me of the sanctity of the threshold.

> *God of Beginnings, accept this offering,*
> *sweet-smelling incense to make you glad.*
> *Bless me on the beginning of this year,*
> *and bless my beginnings throughout this year.*

☽ ○ ☾

> *God of the threshold,*
> *who opens up to a new year;*
> *god of doors,*
> *who opens onto a new time;*
> *Janus, who looks both ways,*
> *I pour out this wine to you*
> *and ask you to look behind and ahead*
> *and guide me through the year that begins today.*

☽ ○ ☾

A New Year is born from you;
praise, blessings, and honors are due for this gift!
Hear my words, you who give birth to everything.
A newly born year takes its place among your
*   wonders,*
one more thing for which you might rightly be
*   praised.*

Prayer for Brighid's Day (Imbolc)

'Brighid's Day is February 2nd. It makes sense to honor a hearth goddess in the dead of winter, when, in the old times, families would be gathered around the hearth to warm themselves with fire and companionship. This may also be used to bless the stove or fireplace of a new house.

Brighid, Our Lady, queen of our hearth,
goddess who guards the heart of our home,
threefold flame who shines in the center:
we honor and praise you,
we offer you our words of worship.
Queen of Poets, may our lives be creative.
Queen of Smiths, may our lives be useful.
Queen of Healers, may our lives be healthy.
Your family is standing before you here,
confident you will do what is right.

Prayers for Spring

The God and the Goddess

The snow, melting, waters the Earth,
the semen soaking deep into the womb.
Mother and Father, conceive the spring.
Bring to birth the warm time.

The God

Wielder of the flaming arrow,
look down from your place on high,
and, fitting a shaft to your bow,
let loose your bowstring.
Sink deep into the Earth the shaft of fire,
warming the world, bringing the spring.

The Goddess

The snow sinks back into the Earth,
there to nourish the sleeping life
that waits patiently for its time to come.
Goddess of spring, you have performed this miracle
through many ages.
Transform, again, the frozen white into the pliant
green.
Work, again, the ancient magic,
and bring spring to our land.

Demeter

I pray to you, Demeter, to remind you of the spring,
for Persephone has come home to you,
your little girl, now a great queen.
Show us your joy, mother of grain,
at her homecoming.
Warm the Earth, make the ground soft,
so we may walk barefoot again in the grass
and plant the seeds that will grow all summer
until the harvest, when your full power will be known
and everyone will see what you have done.
But now it is the time to begin these great deeds.
Bring us the spring, that together we might produce
      the harvest.
Warm the Earth, that the plants might grow so we
might display your gifts.
With your tears cried for happiness, melt away the
winter's snow
and nourish the waiting seeds.

Eostre

Blessed be Eostre, springtime queen,
blessed in all the signs of warmth's return,
blessed in the scent of thawing Earth,
her own true incense rising up in her praise.

Land Spirits

How silently flowers fall from the trees
and cover the Earth like winter's melted snow.
Like winter's melted snow, they will go on their way,

opening the door to summer's warmth.
Thank you, dear trees, for your gifts of the flowers,
and for the teaching that comes with them on this
day in spring.

☽ ○ ☾

The warm time is here:
time to work and time to rest,
time to celebrate outside,
time to prepare for the harvest.
All about us, the Land Spirits are singing.
All about us, the deities are speaking.
Help me to listen, all you divine beings.
May I hear your voices.

Prayers for Gardening

I will need much help in growing this garden.
I cannot do it alone.
I ask for help from the Sun: give your light so the
plants can make their food.
I ask for help from the rain: give your moisture to be
the plants' own blood.
I ask for help from the soil: give your minerals from
which the plants will form their bodies.
I will give my time,
I will give my care,
I will give my loving stewardship.
All these will I give my garden
and I ask for you others to give what the garden will
need as well.

We will do it together
and I will not forget your contribution.

☽ ○ ☾

Gods of planting and growing,
bless my work today.
Bring together water and soil and seed,
bring to them light and air.
Stir up life with them.
Fill my garden with prosperous growth.

Prayer for Floralia (April 28)

Each flower that stands in all the world's gardens
is a tribute to you, Queen Flora.
Every one that blooms in the wild places of the Earth
is an offering both from and to you.

Prayers for Summer

Summer is a tough time to remember to pray—there are so many good things going on. But then that's all the more reason to do it.

Prayer at the Beach

Lift me up, Mother Ocean, as I enter your waves.
As I swim in you, keep me safe.

[With slight changes, this can become a blessing from a parent to a child before swimming.]

Prayers for July Fourth

Goddess Liberty,
we pray to you today.
Grant freedom to all your children,
no matter their country.
We take time today to remember
the examples of freedom we have seen in our time.
We remember the citizens of Berlin,
who knew that the best use for a wall is to dance
*   upon it.*
We remember the hole in the Romanian flag,
put there by those who overthrew their oppressors.
We remember the people who stood in Russian
Parliament Square
and waited for the tanks to come.
And we remember those who struggled and failed,
such as the martyrs of Tiananmen Square,
who, after raising a statue to you,
faced the tanks and lost.
We will not forget.
We will not forget.
Give us the courage
to earn our freedom
and to regain it if it is stolen.
We ask this of you
who are the source of all freedom.

☽ ○ ☾

Liberty, your torch shines undimmed by the years.
If our eyes have lost sight of you, it is our fault and
   not yours.
We have turned our vision away from the heights
   from which your flames shine,
and seen only that which divides.
Be our beacon, Mother of our nation,
and show us the way again.
Mother of Peoples,
unite your scattered children into one tribe,
one people, one country.

Prayers for Lammas

The God

The feast of bread we celebrate with bread
baked and on our table to be shared among us,
but first to be shared with the Lord of Grain.
And so I break off this piece and pass it among you.
Bless it, each who is here,
that it may be the holy which we share with the holy,
placing it in the [field/garden];
and sharing the rest,
eating together with the Holy One.
And this second loaf we give,
turning it over wholly,
after blessing it, each one of us,
separating it out for him alone.
And then we will place it, as well, in the [field/
   garden].
We are grateful to you, Grain God,

we send you our blessings.
Look kindly on us, King of Bread,
and continue to send us blessings in return.

Earth Mother

Bread lain on the ground,
on which we scatter grain.
We offer to the Earth
in thanks for the gift of the harvest
on the feast day of bread.

Prayers for Lughnasadh

Lugh

Withhold your lightning spears, Lugh whose own is
  true,
until the harvest is safely gathered in
against the dark and cold which must come,
god of the bright and hot, hear the words of one who
  loves you.

☽ ○ ☾

You who brought Bres low,
who won from him the secrets of planting,
who won from him the secrets of growth,
who won for him the secrets of harvest,
it is at harvest that we pray to you
it is today that we pray to you, your holy day,
Lughnasadh, that is to say, festival of Lugh.
We thank you, Lamfada, for your protection,

for watching over our field against all danger,
whether animals who might have eaten our crops
whether humans who might have encroached on our
    land
whether spirits who might have wished us ill:
against all these, Long-Arm, you have defended us
    and ours.
And so to you, guider and protector,
teacher and champion,
we pray on this day,
which is rightly called yours.

Prayers for the Dog Days

In the hot days of August, I am reminded of you
by the Sun-seared grass now brown in my yard.
It is brittle and dead now and provides no comfort
    when I walk across it.
It is life appearing in the semblance of death,
for when the autumn rains come, it will be green again.
Of such small miracles, splendid gods,
is your world made.

☽ ○ ☾

Look! The garden is growing well!
Through your help, and through my work,
we have done a great deed, Holy Ones.
We have produced food from seeds' promise.

Prayer for the Tomato Season

I stop for a moment to praise tomatoes,
honoring them by eating one.
Lovely are you spirits who grow such things.
First I praise their shapes—they shun the easy
     perfection of the sphere
and take instead their own forms.
Their weight is worth praising, and the depth of their
     color.
Before I eat this one, I smell it, taking its scent in
deeply,
finding in me a resonance that tells me that this is
     the smell of fertile Earth.
Their skin, though stretched tightly, yields quickly;
it has performed its duty of containing treasure with
     uncommon devotion
and now relinquishes command to me.
With silent thanks, then, I accept the task
and eagerly receive the honor so bestowed,
hoping, by so doing, to honor in turn the giver of the
     gift
and the gift itself.

Prayer for Summer's End

The door is starting to swing from hot to cold.
Although it is still summer, occasionally a cool
day comes. The pokeberries are purple, the sassafras
is starting to turn, and the gardens are
heavy with tomatoes. It is a time to stop and pay
attention: the spirits of the land are very busy. I
pray to them at this liminal time to open my eyes.

Don't let me wake one day and ask where summer
has gone. May I be aware of its going, and
be as thrilled with it as I was with the arrival of
spring.

☽ ○ ☾

Late in the summer, with the Sun still blazing
I meet with the startling sight of sassafras leaves,
turned already to tongues of flame.
They burn away the remnants of summer,
a sacrificial pyre for the year's offerings,
set to summon the fires of fall.
Spirits of sassafras, many thanks to you:
your message will not go unheeded.

Prayers for Fall

Perhaps the most important thing to pray for in the fall is
to be reminded that it is not so much the beginning of the
cold season so many of us dread, as it is the high point of
the main harvest season. Without fall we would die.

Prayers for the Fall Equinox

I set my face to the dark.
I will travel with the Sun through the dark.
I will go with confidence in the deepest dark.
Though about me the dark may grow,
the gods are always at my side
guiding me to light.

꩜ ○ ☽

This is what I know, gods of the universe.
This is what you are telling me
and this is what I tell you:
the Earth prepares for a great change.
Light and dark are equal today, but that will not last.
The Earth makes its way around the Sun
and takes us with it into the year's dark half.
We travel with it,
not in calm resignation,
but with wild anticipation of what dreams may be
dreamt
in the night of the world.
May they be good dreams.

☽ ○ ☾

The sacrificial fires of maple trees burn the summer
offering,
the grey sky accepting the smoke offered it in honor.
I place this sacrifice before you, gods of the year.
May each death on the point of the cold's sharp
sword
be considered an offering on the altar of the Earth.
May each plant harvested be granted the status of
sacrifice.
May each loss to the end of the year be an addition
to your power,
a thread in the pattern woven by you in the secret
places.[1]

The God

It happened this way:
When the time was right, when the season had
come, he came to the deadly place and was sacrificed.
Knowingly he came, willingly he came, in
honor and sorrow he came, to do what had to be
done.
His death made life possible; from it sprang the food
we eat. Grain grew where his blood flowed, animals
walked forth from the shade of his fallen
body. Like an ash felled by an axe, his body lay
and, with its rotting, nourished the ground.
This is the way it happened, and the way it happens
today.
For each moment dies and nourishes the next as it is
birthed by the Goddess. Each year dies and nourishes
the next as it is birthed by the Goddess. Each life
ends and nourishes the next as it is
birthed by the Goddess.
You who die and are reborn, in this season of death
we remember your deeds.
You who die and are reborn, in this season of life we
remember your sacrifice.
You who die and are reborn, in this season of life
and death we remember what happened, and
we praise you in our living, and we praise you in
our dying.

The Goddess

Never will I say, Queen of the Earth,
that your power has ever been diminished.
Today, I saw leaves flying in the wind
and they told me not to doubt.
Though the strong gusts strip the trees of their
summertime finery
and empty branches reach black against the twilight
sky,
my heart will not shudder,
nor my spirits fail.
You are the guide to whom the events of the world
look
and they do not stray from the path you are
continually laying down:
this autumn that transforms the world is a return to
autumns past.
Standing among the fallen leaves,
I praise you,
I pray to you,
I bring to mind your glory.

Meal Prayer for Early Fall

With longer shadows, I sit down to my supper.
Before me are the products of summer,
the Sun's light become food.
Listen, food and Sun:
I thank you.

Prayers for the Hunting Season

Hunting is a source of some controversy among neo-Pagans. Our respect for life has led some of us to reject hunting. I doubt that any would approve of hunting simply for trophies. And yet, what about hunting for food? If we are to eat meat, we owe it to the animals who die for us to make their deaths a sacred act. It is doubtful that a worker in a slaughterhouse will do this for us. Those who hunt, however, have a chance to take part in the dance of life and death. A properly prayerful attitude makes hunting a sacred act. Through prayer a hunter is reminded that what they hunt is sacred, and that the God was himself the victim of a hunt. (This is a myth that is implicit in various forms of the myth of the year.) The hunter then puts themselves and their actions under the control of the God. In essence, it is the God who will be hunting. In this way the hunter takes the part of the God as hunter, but in the back of their mind is the thought that, as they are the God, so are they the hunted as well.

*The flame on the trees burns away the green of
    summer.
Summer's last heat is put to good use.
Run with the prey as hunting time starts,
race through the forest with the deer, god of stags.
The blood on the ground, as red as the leaves that
    fall on it,
flows from your sacrifice as this season is born.
In autumn, the dying time, you come into your own;
the day comes round for your greatest of gifts.
Lord of flame and blood, lord of deer and sacrifice,
Lord of autumn and gifts, bless your people.*

Is it true what they say about you,
Great Lord of Animals?
Is it true that you know what it is to be hunted,
to be sought by those who would take your life?
I hear that, at the end, you turned to face them,
at the moment you knew the time was right,
and stood, a willing sacrifice for the people,
awaiting your death.
May it be thus today, Beast Lord.
May no animal come before my weapon except as
*   you will.*
May no animal be taken by me except in the
moment that is right.
May we never forget that it is death that feeds our
lives.

[This prayer is an example of what can be done to sanctify the death of a hunted animal.]

Prayer for Late Fall

Lock up carefully, Earth's guardians,
and keep life safe until spring.

Prayer for Comfort

Wild geese flying overhead on your journey south,
bear away with you on your thundering wings
the cares that have made my summer weary.
Cry out my pain, passing over the darkened land,
until the air ocean you sail washes it away.

CHAPTER 13

PRAYERS FOR THE TIMES OF LIFE

Just as the changes in nature outside of us deserve to be honored with prayer, so do the changes within us; we are part of nature too.

Prayers for New Life

Prayers for Pregnancy

> *My words to all the gods:*
> *which of you watches over this child?*
> *Who will protect her, during her whole life?*
> *Whom should she worship to ask for this help?*
> *Who will be fit for her to worship when she is old*
>   *enough?*
> *I await your answer.*[1]

☽ ○ ☾

> *[Patron Deity], I am undergoing a great task,*
> *one I gratefully accept.*
> *Be my strength in this time.*

[Household deity], a new one has come into our
*   family,*
welcome her and protect her until her birth.
All the gods and goddesses, your people are
*   increased.*
Rejoice with me; a new life has come.

The Goddess

Each moment you experience this,
you who bring each moment through to its proper
*   time.*
This is my first pregnancy, however,
and I lean on you, asking for strength.
During the time of growing, give me strength.
Guide the baby in the way it is to grow,
bring it to health and strength.
During the time of waiting, give me patience,
so that my pregnancy might reach its fulfillment in
*   its proper time.*
You are my model, Mater Dea,
and I look to you for help.

The Matronae

Matronae Three, sitting so gently,
I will need both gentleness and strength in the days
*   ahead.*
Aid me as I become a mother:
You know well what that means.
May I know also.

Prayer for a Soon-to-be Father

I stand on the outside, Mother.
I do not feel the changes, only see them.
I am dismayed, Mother;
I don't know what to do and my body won't tell me.
You will have to tell me so I can help your daughter.
Teach me, Mother, how to be a father.

Prayers for Birth

Stand about her, servants of the Mother,
singing the birth songs clearly
so that the baby, although deep inside,
may learn what it must know
to do what it must do.
Go before her, Way-Shower,
open the gates, open the doors,
open all ways, that the birth might be easy.

☽ ○ ☾

The child moves down the birth canal
on the first of its many journeys.
[Mother goddess] may its journey be smooth and
safe.

Aurora

Aurora,
herald the dawn of this new life.

Prayers for Parenthood

> *Holy Ones, see what has happened here!*
> *I have become a [[father, mother];*
> *a great mystery indeed.*
> *I do not know in my head what to do,*
> *I know in my heart what is right.*
> *May I know the right thing with all of me*
> *and do it no matter what the pain.*
> *A hard road lies before me, shining ones,*
> *a road filled with great difficulties,*
> *a road filled with great joys.*
> *Guide me along it.*
> *Be at my side.*

The God

> *Father of Worlds, I turn to you in prayer*
> *that you might bless me, my father,*
> *who took your role here on Earth and performed it*
>   *well.*
> *May I act the role as artfully!*

Prayers for Childhood and Growth

Since I wrote a book on practicing Paganism with children, it should come as no surprise that children's prayers interest me. Prayers are an important introduction to our religion. They contain principles of belief and guides for conduct, and provide a healthy example of the proper relationship between the gods and people. Through them, children may first come to experience the sacred, something that will sustain them through their whole life. Don't just pray for your children, then; pray with them.

Prayers for Infancy

> *May the gods walk beside this child throughout her*
> *   life,*
> *guiding her steps into the way proper to her,*
> *guiding her way along the sacred path.*

The God and the Goddess

> *On this baby who rests in my arms,*
> *pour blessings, O Lord, pour blessings.*
> *On this baby who rests in my arms,*
> *pour blessings, O Lady, pour blessings.*

Ancestors

> *Spirits of the Ancestors, do you see what has been done?*
> *A child has been born to continue your line.*
> *Once again, a link is forged in the ancient chain*
> *and we are all connected that much tighter.*
> *Bless this child, then;*
> *she carries your memory forward to the future.*

☽ ○ ☾

> *We bring before you today one of yours, people of*
> *our past,*
> *one who will continue what you started in the long*
> *ago time.*

She is one of us, one of the family that reaches so far back,
and we will need to guide her until she is ready to assume her full responsibilities.
Be with her and us as we do that; as she grows, be at her side to help.
Come to us today to learn who she is,
come and celebrate with us.

Parents' Prayers for Their Children

Today my child took her first step.
May it be the first step on the path of the gods.
Open the way for her, you who love her,
guide her, protect her, walk beside her.

Hera

Keep an eye on my daughter, Hera,
as the day goes by,
whether I am with her or not.

Prayers for a Sick Child

[Patron deity], your child is ill.
Bring her to health.
I pledge you an offering of [offering] when she is well.

☽ ○ ☾

Eternal Balance, see what I place before you,
listen to the story I tell:
there is a disturbance here, something that should
    not be.
A child is sick. How can this be?
You know that the business of childhood is growing.
Yet sickness prevents growth.
How can it be, then, that this child is sick?
Perhaps you were sleeping and did not notice.
I have brought it to your attention now,
and I know you will do what is right.
Eternal Balance, Continuous Harmony,
I place my child in your arms for healing.

Children's Prayers

May I always walk carefully on the path of the gods
with my eyes and ears open to their teachings.

The God and Goddess

As I grow and learn,
help me, O Mother,
help me, O Father,
to know what is right
and to do only that.

☽ ○ ☾

I have a mother and I have a father.
They have mothers, and they have fathers.
We all have mothers, we all have fathers.

And we all have the Mother, and we all have the
Father,
Our Goddess and God, to keep us safe.

Hermes

Hermes, tricky one,
even as a child you were clever.
Help me with this problem.

Ogmios

Ogmios, god of learning,
guide me in school today.
Keep my mind open
and fill it with learning.

Land Spirits

Land Spirits, show yourself to me
and teach me to love nature.

Prayers for Puberty

Balanced on the knife blade,
you come to me for blessing.
And I, your father, say this:
Be true. Be strong. Keep your promises.
Seek wisdom. Love your friends.
Be at peace. Bless your children.
This is my blessing to you.
May all the Holy Ones help you to make it true.

At this time of great change, I tell you a hard truth:
you are the one who must undergo this task.
I cannot do it for you, nor can any others do it for you.
Your magic lies within.
You know what to do.
Look deeply and you will see.
A hard time lies before you, but you go under the
    protection of the Holy Ones
and you go guarded by our love.
Gods of clear sight,
Goddesses of the fierce change,
help your daughter in what she must do.
Be beside her, be with her, be her unfailing aid.
Help her to do what she must.

Prayers for Weddings

May the blessings of all the world descend on this couple:
the blessings of Earth, the blessings of sky,
the blessings of the moving ocean and of the never-
    still wind.
From the people of stone, blessings;
the blessings of plants and the blessings of animals;
of two-legged and four, of six and of eight;
and the blessings of the footless ones.
From all those who dwell on the Earth
and in it and above it,
may blessings flow.

I pray to you, goddess of weddings,
who for so long presided over these happy rites.
We call to you again;
awake, come to us,
and once more shower blessings
on those who come before you.

The God and Goddess

On this couple who stand before you,
pour blessings, Holy Ones, Divine Pair,
that their union may be as strong as yours,
lasting through all ages.

☽ ○ ☾

That there might be love, she formed him
and drew him to herself.
And he, with newly opened eyes,
knew with clear sight his true fate.
And she, with her heart's own true wisdom,
knew that love had passed expectations.
They loved, they love, they will love.
Blessings on love and on all who love.
Blessings from the gods and goddesses of love.

Dionysos

Dionysos, god not only of bliss,
but of faithful and dedicated love,
be both my model and my guide
in my life as a husband.

Juno

Marriage guardian, Juno,
wife of Jupiter Greatest and Best,
protector, mother, queen:
I pray to you on my wedding day
to make my marriage as wonderful as this day.

Prayers for Dying

I am not so out of touch with reality that I think that a dying person can necessarily say these prayers. They can, however, be said on someone's behalf, guiding them home.

At the end of my life, I put my trust in the gods of my
    people.
Ancient Wise Woman, cover me with your cloak
as I walk the last path that leads to your land.

☽ ○ ☾

Lord of Death, I will greet you soon with arms wide
    open in trust
as I cross the boundary into your realm.
I will enter the world beyond worlds
with my eyes open and my head lifted,
ready to experience its unique wonders,
no less beautiful than in this world I have known.
I will go to the Land of Youth,
to rest in your halls, O gods of my people,

to commune with the spirits of those who have gone
this way
and who wait for me, there on the other side.

☽ ○ ☾

Fearful One, when I see your face,
may it be without fear,
may it be without terror,
may it be without panic.
Old Woman, when I see your face,
may it be with understanding,
may it be with courage,
may it be with peace.
Aged One, when I see your face,
may I be brought to wisdom
through your loving kindness.

☽ ○ ☾

First one to die,
to you I pray.
To you I call,
as you sit between this world and the next:
God of the in-between,
to you my words go out.
As I approach the moment of my death,
as I come closer to the point of transformation,
as I grow nearer to the time of ending,
I ask your help.
Grant me the courage to do what I must do.
Grant me the wisdom to understand its necessity.
Grant me the peace that you have found,
the peace that is found in the land between the
worlds.[2]

Prayer for the Recently Dead

You are journeying across the dividing water that lies
between this world and the next,
carried away by the ferryman on your way.
Look ahead of you, do not look behind.
Look ahead of you, where your destiny lies.
Do you see them? They are there, ahead of you on
the other shore.
Slowly, they become visible to you;
the shining ones appear slowly out of the concealing
mists.
Clearly they appear to you, though hidden from our
eyes.
Go to them, they welcome you.
Go to them, not stopping for farewells.
Holy Ones in the world beyond,
open wide your arms to receive this one who is
journeying to you.
Make him a home, bring him to rest.
Farewell, [name].
We who have loved you wish you a good journey.

Prayers for Funerals

Open the way, Lord of Death,
for this one to travel.
Be his guide, show him the right path,
which you yourself traveled in the before time.
You who blazed the trail, leaving your marks behind,
teach him the signs to follow.

Make the road clear, removing the blocks.
Speed him on his way to your home.
Accept him into your land.

The Goddess

Mother of All, absorb the spirit of our loved one
back into your womb from which he was born.
There, reshape him in your place of molding,
preparing him for rebirth among his people.

Charon

Old Man, ferry this one across safely,
bringing him swiftly and without detour
to the other side of the great sea.
Pole your boat here to this place and perform your
     duty.
His fare is paid, his place secured,
so take him aboard and carry him away,
over the sea, following the setting Sun,
to the landing place before the great city
where the Lord of Death rules.
Bring this one before he who sits on his throne.
Make his name known to the ruler there.
Make smooth the way, open the doors,
clear the path, unlock the gates.
Charon, this one is starting on a great journey.
Stand by him until he is safely home!

Yama

Lord of the enclosed land,
ruler of the flowery plain,
Yama who first took this path:
bring this one home.
May he flourish in the land beyond.
May he be happy in your land of joy.
May he rest, may he rest.

Ancestors

Go your way to the land of the Ancestors,
where they wait for you with open arms,
there on the edge between this world and the next.
See; there they stand.
Ancestral spirits, welcome this one
to the place where we all must go.

CHAPTER 14

PETITIONARY PRAYERS AND BLESSINGS

Petitionary prayers ask for things. People are often criticized for petitioning through prayer. In fact, it is because of this kind of prayer that prayer in general is most often criticized. That's why I saved this chapter for late in the book; I wanted to show just how many other ways one could pray before raising the question of petitions.

The usual objection is that petitionary prayers reduce religion to a cosmic "gimme." We ask the gods and they give, and if they don't, we lose faith in them and turn to other gods or spirits. This makes the gods our flunkies who have to toady to us if they know what's good for them.

Petitionary prayer can be so much more than this, though, if it is approached properly. I have already discussed prayers of thanksgiving and praise. These go a long way toward creating a good relationship with the gods. Praise shows the gods, and reminds you, that you appreciate the gods, that you don't see them as your employees. Thanksgiving shows the gods, and reminds you, that you don't consider what you ask for to be your right, something they have to give you.

One way to prevent the "gimme" attitude that is not acceptable is to limit petitionary prayers to intangible things. Some of the prayers in this chapter ask for what might be described as material blessings—fertility, prosperity, health. Others ask for what might be called spiritual blessings—comfort, awareness, wisdom. It is one of the teachings of Paganism, however, that the material is no less valuable than the spiritual. As Pagans, we do not point our noses to the sky and say, "Well, I only pray for spiritual things." The material is just as sacred as the spiritual.

Nor do we pray for an excess of things. Excess is a drain on the Earth. Pagans try not to be a drain on anything—not if they are true to their path, that is.

Pray for what is right, for what is good, for what is deserved, and let no one but the gods tell you that it is wrong.

Miscellaneous Petitionary Prayers

All the gods of my people:
hear me.
Let it be your words I write.
Let it be your words I speak.

☽ ○ ☾

This time in which I find myself is no less sacred
than the times of the Ancestors when the laws were
laid down.

This place in which I find myself is no less sacred
than the circles of stone beneath faraway skies.
I pray to all the beings that dwell in this world,
to stone and tree, to waves and breezes,
to person and beast, to deities and dust motes:
do not let me forget.
Keep my eyes open
to the sacred that surrounds me
and in which I live.

☽ ○ ☾

Around me, all the gods of the land are watching—
May I do what is right.

☽ ○ ☾

I give from my own store to you,
the gods of this place.
Remember my generosity and be my friends.

☽ ○ ☾

Accept this gift, Holy Ones,
and keep me in your minds,
as I will keep you in my heart.

☽ ○ ☾

Holy Ones, Mighty Ones, I ask for your blessings
      today,
that I might be blessed with holiness and with
      fortune,
that my family might be blessed with holiness and
      with fortune,

that my community might be blessed with holiness
and with fortune,
that my country might be blessed with holiness and
with fortune,
that my planet might be blessed with holiness and
with fortune.
Send them forth, you who are holy.
Send them forth, you filled with fortune.
Send them forth, upon all for whom I pray.
Send them forth, send them forth.

☽ ○ ☾

Blessed one, come near to me and hear my prayer.
You who have, since ancient times, listened to my
people's words,
hear my prayer now.
Great is your power, and perfectly is it applied,
with artful skill, with respect for beauty.
My own might is little indeed;
yours is beyond imagining.
Use your power in my interests:
grant me my wishes, accomplish my objectives.

☽ ○ ☾

I place myself today in the hands of the gods,
knowing that their protection comes with a price.
For those who wish the help of the old ones
must walk their path with all their hearts.
This I promise I will do.

☽ ○ ☾

*Even the stones make it clear to me that everything
partakes of the nature of the gods.
The buildings that surround me speak of the skills
that have been given to us by the gods in ancient
    times,
that are being given to us in these days,
that will always be given to us
by the mighty ones.
Remind me of this daily, you who give so much.*[1]

☽ ○ ☾

*Listen to me, you who grant wisdom:
The stories that have been told about you from the
times when our race was young have taught me
that you are the clearest of thinkers and the best
at deciding the proper path.
I find myself now with a choice to make and I do not
know how to make it. Without a clear road before
me, then, I turn to you for help.
Path-Marker, Way-Shower, what should I do? I ask
that you give me a sign to help me decide. Come
to me with your clear counsel; come to me with
advice. Come to me, whether in a dream, or in
the chance remark of a stranger, or in my own
deliberations. May my decision reflect your calm
wisdom, and my life become thereby a pleasure
for you to see.*

[The exact deity to whom this is directed will depend on your tradition.]

☽ ○ ☾

Spirits of the elements, I stand in your center, a
being that shares in all your ways;
hear me, help me.
Spirits of the land, I praise the land's beauty, and I
do not separate myself from it;
hear me, help me.
Spirits of the Ancestors, I continue to walk the path
you laid down;
hear me, help me.
Deities of my people, I worship you with words and
actions, as from ancient times;
hear me, help me.
All of the numinous beings that crowd about me, I
am a fellow traveler on the ancient path;
Hear me, help me.
Hear me and help me, shining ones,
you who do not cease from watching:
send me aid when it is most needed.

☽ ○ ☾

Sweet gods and goddesses,
give me the right words to say.
Inspiring Brighid, eloquent Sarasvati,
skillful Daghda, Lugh of smooth speech,
Hermes of the tricking and tripping tongue:
pick out from the many words just the right ones for
this occasion
and feed them to me.
I will do the rest.

☽ ○ ☾

A mighty bull in the field,
a penetrating mind at work:
choosing the appropriate mode, you find no opposition.
Lord of talents, be with me in my efforts.
Bring my plans to fruition.

The God

As coins pouring from your lap,
rain down your gifts on me, Prosperous One.
As plants turning green in spring,
bring prosperity into my life, Lord of Fertility.
As cattle returning to the pastures,
send riches into my life, Great Bull.

☽ ○ ☾

Walk beside me, Lord of Strength,
as I undergo trial.

☽ ○ ☾

Controller of the riches beneath the Earth,
fertilizer of all life upon it,
distributor of the wealth that arises from it:
Lord of the Earth, Lord of Wealth,
when sharing out your bounty,
do not forget me, who am faithful in your service.

The Goddess

Mother, help me,
I am calling to you!
My need is great, but your power is greater.
I know you will prevail over the troubles that beset me.

You who gave birth to all things,
give birth to what I desire;
bring it to pass.

☽ ○ ☾

Thinking carefully, attempting clarity, I ask the
Goddess for inspiration.

Agni

Lord of undying fire that burns within us all,
my prayer is sent to you, from my heart to yours.
As you are enflamed, so may I be also;
filled with the fire that rolls out from your hidden
*   home,*
that golden-walled palace enclosed by living water.
Burn away my weaknesses.
Light within me a raging fire of strength.
Cause me to burn with zeal to perform the acts of the
*   gods.*

Apollo

God of eloquence, teach me to pray.
Open my mouth that the words might come forth.
Open my heart that the words might ring true.

Brighid

May I be filled with the fire of Brighid,
the threefold queen who inspires the [artist, writer,
craftsman, healer, etc.].

Cernunnos

Lord Cernunnos, opener of the door,
guide to the ways between,
gatekeeper of the gods,
open for me the pathway,
that all I wish for might be accomplished.

$$\mathdollar \; ☽ \; ○ \; ☾$$

Cernunnos, lord, sitter in the doorway,
god of equilibrium, terrible, merciful:
you who hold the opposites apart,
you in whom all opposites unite,
my prayer goes to you to open the passage,
to clear the threshold,
to make the way clear.

Fortuna

With the next turn of the wheel, Fortuna,
bring me luck.

Gaṇeśa

Pom, pom, your footfalls shake the trees,
your weighty head forcing trunks and tendrils aside,

> your tusks cutting through foliage, making a way.
> Gaṇeśa, Gaṇeśa, open the way for me.
> Gaṇeśa, Gaṇeśa, remove my obstacles.
> Gaṇeśa, Gaṇeśa, carry me on your back,
> bringing me through difficulties to success.

Hathor

> Heavenly Cow,
> rain your blessings down on your people,
> like milk pouring from above.[2]

Moon

> Throughout the day, you will be observing my actions:
> help me to make them worthy of your notice.
> You who measure the sky, dividing it into sections,
> do not be too strict in your judgment.
> Friend of the honest, be my friend.[3]

Sun

> As spears, as swords, as arrows,
> the Sun sends out his rays,
> as weapons from the hands of a mighty warrior,
> to strike down falsehood and untrue ways.
> As spears, as swords, as arrows,
> Send out your rays,
> as weapons from the hands of a mighty warrior,
> to strike down falsehood and untrue ways.

Viṣṇu

Hail to the Measurer, who laid things out,
putting this one here and that one there,
putting each in the place it belonged.
Hail to the determining one, who established laws,
that all things might run smoothly,
that all things might perform well.
God of establishing, I pray to you:
may you fashion the world in such a way
as to bring me happiness,
as to bring me prosperity,
as to bring me peace,
as to bring blessings on all of your worshippers.

Ancestors

Mother and Fathers who went before,
Watch over my words as I tell the old stories,
that they may be passed on rightly.
Make me today's link in the chain that reaches on,
from nights around the fire beneath African skies
to the end of humanity
and beyond.

Earth Spirits

Do you hear me, Earth spirits,
as I go walking?
Do you hear my footfalls,
drumming on the dirt?
Do you hear my breathing,
mixing with the air?

Do you hear my heart beating,
weaving in the rhythms?
Do you hear my words of prayer,
asking your attention?
Do you hear me, Earth spirits?
Hear me, hear me, hear my voice.
Hear the one who walks among you.
Hear my words of peace and friendship.
Hear my plea, grant my wish.

Civic Prayers

One of the functions of ancient Paganism often overlooked by secularized neo-Pagans is how it provides a support for the social order. As citizens of a country that supports religious freedom, we, of course, do not want to establish any religion, even our own, as official. However, as citizens of a country that supports religious freedom, we should take our religion into our civic duties, and we should gladly seek to support and to guide our country's institutions with prayer.

I pray to all the gods my people worship, and I ask this:
May what is done be done well.
May what is done be done rightly.
May what is done be done according to justice.
May truth prevail, may falsehood fail,
May words and deeds and thoughts be just.

☽ ○ ☾

May all the gods of my people hear my prayers;
as we go to the polls to choose our leaders,
may it be with wisdom.

The God and Goddess

Lady and Lord, bless my country.
Guide its governors, show them the path to take,
make their actions conform to the way of nature.
Knit together the many peoples into one tribe;
unite us, make us a family, as indeed we are under
*   your loving gaze.*

$$\mathbb{D} \bigcirc \mathbb{C}$$

King and Queen of the company of the gods,
rulers of the ruling ones,
inspire those who govern us to do the right things,
the necessary things,
and not just the convenient things.
Grant them the vision to bring peace and justice,
drawing wisdom from the ways of the past
without being bound by them,
looking toward the future with clear eyes.

$$\mathbb{D} \bigcirc \mathbb{C}$$

When I look at the people who stream by me in the
*   city today,*
I do not see my people.
I see the other, the foreigner, the stranger, the
*   unknown, the barbarian.*
I know that this is not right, and still I find I am
*   doing it.*
How will I escape my trap of exclusion, Holy Ones?
How will I learn who my tribe is?
How will I come to know that my family is passing

before me, and I stand by, not only not knowing, but
    actually
preventing that knowledge from coming to my mind?
I pray to you, you who are the parents of this family
of which I am a part:
open my eyes, open my ears, open my mind, open
my heart to all the relatives that surround me.

Hermes

Lord of travelers, unite this land.
We share one road, with many branches:
guide us along it to find each other's homes.
And when we find them, clear our sight
so that we might see that we all live in the same
    neighborhood,
that none of us lives apart.

Mithra

In this case I bring before the court,
may it be your side that I argue, Mithra.
Bring me to the truth, and show me the way to
    proclaim it.
May it not be the side of the more skillful that
    prevails,
but that of the more deserving of justice.
Great Judge, sit in judgment on this case!

☽ ○ ☾

I swear an oath today to Mithra, bringer of justice,
that I will tell only that which is true.

Whether it be to my advantage or bring me harm,
what I say will be what I know to be true.

☽ ○ ☾

Lord of the pledged word
and keeper of oaths:
Mithra, I pray to you for justice.

Prayers for a Jury Member

Ma'at

May my discernment be yours, Ma'at,
as I weigh what I have heard.
In one pan of the balance, may there be always your
feather.

☽ ○ ☾

Against all that is, balances the feather of truth;
Ma'at sits in the balance,
I sit in the other pan.
What I will do will be what is right,
What I will do will equal the truth.

Healing Prayers

Asklepios

You lift your snake-entwined staff, great healer,
and send out healing knowledge.
You know each drug and its effects,

each technique and when it should be used,
each symptom and what it means,
each illness and how to treat it,
each patient and what to do.
May my hands be yours.[4]

Brighid

I pray today to the Lady of Fire,
great Brighid, Triple Goddess.
There is someone here who needs you,
someone who is sick.
I ask you to bring your healing flame,
the warmth of life, into him,
burning away all that is making him sick,
that I might always have cause to praise you.

Prayers for Travelers

Guide us to the right path,
protector of the way.
Steer us toward the proper goal,
guardian of the path.
Open the road that should be traveled to us,
Lord of going.[5]

☽ ○ ☾

May you walk with me,
as I go on my way,
walking yourself in front,
clearing the way.

Guide to travelers,
for your help I pray,
that you might be with me
as I go on my way.

☽ ○ ☾

I give greetings to the gods of this place,
I, a traveler, offer up prayers.
From my land to this one, I have come,
meaning no harm to any who dwell here.
Land Spirits, I pray to you;
though I do not yet know you, I honor you.

☽ ○ ☾

Lord of Trees, I pray to you as I enter this forest.
Watch over my steps while I am under your care.

Poseidon

Poseidon, Earth-Shaker, Lord of the Sea,
your undeniable power moves against this ship,
which moves, in response, from side to side.
This great ship, proud accomplishment of human
mind and muscle, is at your mercy.
We who sail on the surface of your depths
acknowledge your power, and your mastery of this
    realm.
That is why we turn our prayers toward you,
to the blue-maned deep-dweller,
who can stretch out his trident-armed hand

and make the flat sea-surface grow mountains and
    canyons,
foundering the ships that cross it,
or who can, if he wishes, still the churning,
and smooth the way of the wave-cleaving ships.
Lord of waters, we pray to you,
scattering offerings overboard.
Take them and not us.
Receive them gladly and give in return
calm seas and safe passage,
until we return to land
with gratitude for your kindness.

Woden

All-Father Woden, protector of travelers,
guard us, guide us,
bring us through
in safety and ease
on our journey today.

Prayer before Flying

As I enter your realm, spirits of air,
as I mount to the clouds in this airplane,
I place myself in your hands.
There, among the vagaries of the winds,
I won't be afraid, because I know you are my allies.
As I fly today, be at my side.
Protect me until I land again safely.

Prayer for Military Flyers

Ride beneath their planes, protecting spirits,
raising up their wings with your own.
Guide their weapons, warrior spirits,
bringing them to their targets with accuracy.
Be with them throughout their mission, spirits of
   power,
that what must be done will be done,
that it will be done well.

Prayer for a Business Trip .

May I go and return in safety.
May I go and return with profit.
May I go and return accomplishing my goals.
May I go and return in the hands of the gods.
May I go and return under their protection.

Commuter's Prayer

Cernunnos

Remind me on my drive that my anger harms me
more than that which angers me.
Lord of peace, in ultimate calm sitting,
pass on to me some of your beatific pose.
May even my commute be done in beauty.[6]

Prayer after Moving

Land folk, I am here, newly arrived to this place.
I have come from my previous home,
where I lived under the protecting gaze
of the Land Spirits there.
In this new place, then, I wish to establish peace again
between my people and the people of the land,
as it has been done since the unremembered time.
I bring gifts to you, I bring offerings,
as a suppliant should when entering a chieftain's hall.
Accept them from me and, with them, my friendship.
Establish between us peace.

Prayers for Protection

Encompass me about with your protection,
Holy Ones of old.
Stand about me on all sides,
warding away from me all dangers,
keeping away from me all harm.

☽ ○ ☾

Stand about me, you protective spirits,
on all six sides establish your guards.
From all dangers, no matter from what quarter,
whether from above or below, keep me safe.

The God and Goddess

My Lord at my right hand, my Lady at my left:
be with me throughout my life,
watching over me by night and by day.

The Goddess

Your arms are strong, Mother;
they can hug a child
or restrain one from harm.
Wrap them about me:
I trust you to know which is needed.

Apollo

Your bow's swift arrows:
are they of blessing or destruction?
Show your blasting face to those who need it.
Show your blessing face to those who deserve it.
Whether beating down mercilessly
or shining benevolently,
bring what is right to each, Apollo.
Whether by fighting off enemies
or singing them to peace,
be my protector
and I will always speak sweetly of you.

Guan Yin

Guan Yin of the gentle hands,
with arms held wide in benediction:
come between my enemies and me
and join us together in peace.

Isis

Goddess with the enfolding wings,
wrap them about me, Isis; keep fear and danger at
*   bay.*
May I mount your throne and rest there in peace.

$$☽ ○ ☾$$

Queen Isis, wrap your wings about my family and
*   me*
and bring us through danger in safety.

Moon

You move among the stars as a shepherdess among
*   her sheep,*
guiding them, keeping them from straying.
Mother Moon, softly light my way,
keeping me from danger as well.

Rudra

Turn aside your storms, send them away.
May peace descend in their wake.
Rager, Rudra, Lord of Lightning,

withhold your chaos,
pass by this place, leaving it in calm.

[Sometimes it is appropriate to pray to a deity to stay away. Perhaps if you ask politely, they will listen.]

Spider Woman

Spider Woman, weaver of beauty;
Spider Woman, laying patterns on the world;
Spider Woman, binding all things together:
wrap your threads lightly about me in protection.

Storm God

Striker, axe-bearer, splitter, hammerer:
protect me.
Bolt-caster, cleaver, smasher, way-clearer:
protect me.
Warrior, victor, overcomer, protector:
protect me.

☽ ○ ☾

Break their shields, hammerer;
dissolve their defenses, stormer;
remove their courage, thunderer.
Fight beside me as my comrade,
win through with me to victory.

[This prayer is as appropriate in the boardroom as on the battlefield.]

☽ ○ ☾

With your quick-sent lightning and penetrating rain,
make the Earth fertile, storm-rider, hammer-wielder.

☽ ○ ☾

Wield the lightning on my side, Thunderer,
and I will ensure that my cause is just.

Thor

Wielder of the hammer,
red-bearded one,
Thor, protector,
to you I call.
I stand in the midst of a storm
and ask your protection.

☽ ○ ☾

You who bear the flaming hammer,
to you I pray:
fight on my side against all my opponents.
For with you on my side, who can stand before me?
Remember my devotion to you, Lord of Thunder.
As I work to your honor, may you work also to mine.[7]

Prayers for Comfort

The God and Goddess

May I not forget in the midst of despair
that all things are born from the Goddess and God,
so that even the trials that come to afflict me
are the children of those who are my blessed parents.

The God

He walks at my side,
armed with sword and staff,
and in the darkest of nights,
my fears fly before him.
He looks into my eyes,
sitting with empty hands,
and in the brightest of days,
my cares are as nothing.

☽ ○ ☾

I raise my hands in prayer to the God,
to him I pray, Lord of the Earth.
He who was the first of any to die,
the first of any to be reborn.
He who rises with the Sun each day
and sets with it each night.
Out of my darkness and death, I call
and pray to you,
Lord of All.
Out of my need, I send my voice
with honor and longing,
in hope of intercession.
Grant me my prayer, Mighty One,
you who know what it is to suffer.
Grant me my prayer, Antlered One,
you who are the great giver.

☽ ○ ☾

God of justice, may I not complain
at what fate has brought to me.

Cleave my night with your lightning-axe,
dividing my troubles into ones I can bear.

The Goddess

With your soothing fingers,
wipe away the lines that worries have etched on our
     faces.
Surround us with calm,
let us rest in the glow of peace,
as if we were encircled with the Moon's own light.
Let our concerns and tensions drain away from us,
pouring as water into your Earth.
Accept our troubles
and transform them into wonders.

☽ ○ ☾

I drop my fears into your ocean
and watch them sink from sight.
I place my fears on your broad Earth
and see them rot away.
I put my fears into your hands
and they are no more.
When you offer your arms to me,
Great Mother,
your hands hold nothing but love.

Cernunnos

In the center of the storm, there is calm.
In the center of confusion, there is peace.
In the center of exhaustion, there is rest.

Cernunnos, sitting in the midst of the world,
lead me to the center
and grant me the calm and peace and rest that is
    found there.

Isis

Queen Isis, my lady, my goddess,
since ancient times the bringer of comfort,
who mourned for your husband the Lord Osiris:
be with me now in my time of loss.
Grieve with me now in my time of loss.
Comfort me now in my time of loss.
Wrap about me your soothing wings,
Blankets to warm me from sorrow's cold hands.

Zurvan Akarana

Zurvan Akarana, to you I call, from the turning
    world,
toward the center I face you,
who stand like a pillar in the still point,
enwrapped with the turning,
surrounded by the changing.
It all happens about you;
you are not aloof from it,
you are there in its midst.
You do not reject the changing world,
nor do you transcend it,
but by standing within it, you find the still point.
Axis mundi, to you I call, from the turning world.
May I, though engrossed in the great changing,
find, even as you, the center.

Bird Spirit

> *Hey, you up there,*
> *you, bird up there,*
> *up there, bird.*
> *Look down here.*
> *Look and see me,*
> *me down here.*
> *Take my cares away from here.*
> *Away from here, far away.*

[Land Spirits often manifest themselves in bird form; deities sometimes do as well.]

Prayers for Work

Athena

> *Sprung full-armed from the head of Zeus*
> *with fully formed faculties,*
> *nimble Athena, who guides the craftsman:*
> *turn me onto a productive path.*

Coyote

> *Hey you, Coyote,*
> *thanks for your gifts.*
> *Don't forget to keep on giving.*
> *We can always use more.*

Lugh

I sit [stand] before my place of work
and spread my tools before me.
Lugh Samildanach,
grant your blessings on my tools
that they might serve me as well
as the parts of my body do.
Master Craftsman,
grant your blessings upon me,
that my work might bring beauty
to all the world and all who live in it.
Orderer of Chaos,
grant that all that I do might be in accord
with the will of Nature,
so that, by doing my work,
I might do the will of the gods.

Mercury

During today's negotiations, make me eloquent,
Mercury,
ease the way, remove all obstacles,
opening the path for a smoothly accomplished deal,
opening the path for a profitable outcome.

Oghma, Brighid

I take up my pen and invoke Oghma:
God of writing, make my way smooth.
I take up my pen and invoke Brighid:
Inspiring goddess, enflame my words.

Prayers for Divination

Speak to me as you follow the wind,
leaves of oak above my head.
Follow perfectly the waves of the air-ocean,
making known to me their invisible pattern.
Out of the well of the world they flow,
carrying the wisdom that is her gift.
Carry it to me also, give to me, oak spirit,
the knowledge that you have,
the knowledge that I seek.[8]

$$\text{☽ ○ ☾}$$

Weaving goddess, who knows the woof and warp,
who sees the pattern before the cloth exists,
form from my actions here that which will be
if the threads remain as they are now arranged.

Prayer for Relief from a Drought

Sun

The hard Earth lies vulnerable beneath the
    onslaught of the Sun's rays,
too weak from thirst even to raise her hands in
    prayer for relief.
I do it for her, then; I raise my face to the Sun:
shining disk, wheel of light,
your power is indeed great, your place of honor is
    assured.
I come to you as a herald, asking for peace.

> *Withhold your darts that are keeping back the rain*
> > *clouds.*
> *Allow them to come and quench the thirst of their*
> > *sister below.*
> *Establish peace between yourself and the Earth:*
> *a true king knows when to relent.*

Prayer at the End of a Drought

Clouds

> *The sky is weeping great tears in sorrow at the*
> > *Earth's drought.*
> *Weep on, over-reaching clouds:*
> *Your sorrow will return life to the Earth.*

Prayers for the Land Spirits

In general, the divine beings like us. That is one of the reasons they want our prayers and offerings; if they didn't care about us, they wouldn't care about our prayers. That's why they respond well to petitionary prayers; they want to help us. They really do.

Some of them are ambivalent, however. Why should the Land Spirits feel warmly toward us when we cut down their forests and pave over their meadows? Don't feel too smug because you have protested against logging in old growth forest. Where do you think the land your house is built on came from? What kind of land was there before it was plowed under to grow your food?

Dealing with Land Spirits can be difficult. We have to show them we are grateful for their sacrifice. As I hope I have shown earlier in this book, we do this by giving something back.

Here on a stone, in the midst of trees,
I place an offering to the gods of this place.
Though I don't know your names, I know you are here
and I wish for your friendship,
for me and my people.
Accept what I give you
and do not forget me.

☽ ○ ☾

Spirits of this place,
whether you are gods or goddesses,
accept these offerings from one who wishes only to
be at peace with you.
Today I am your host
and I give you a host's gifts.
Tomorrow the turn may fall to you
and you will be the hosts.
Remember that I have acted as hospitality requires,
and reciprocate when the time is right.
May the gods help us always to do
only that which is right.

Prayers for Destruction

Even more scary than the Land Spirits are the deities of destruction and death. Since Paganism seeks to include all life, it must include its bad parts as well as its good. That is not to say that we have to like the bad things. It is certainly OK to ask that they pass us by. But some of it is unavoidable, so we ask for the strength to deal with it. Sometimes we ask benevolent deities to protect us, and sometimes we ask the not-so-benevolent ones to deal lightly with us, or to show us in what way our sufferings are necessary and even valuable.

I don't want to wax poetic about how curses can be blessings in disguise, and I don't want to insult those who suffer by implying that their suffering is a good thing. I do want to say, however, that sometimes suffering can indeed bring blessings. It shows us that the world is not all bunnies, kittens, and rainbows, which means we come face to face with reality, a great blessing. It both tests us and strengthens us. We learn how much we can stand and how to stand worse, if it should come. We learn that sometimes good things are born from bad things. Think of the pain that comes with childbirth. All in all, may the gods protect the person who grows up without experiencing suffering; the first strong wind they encounter as an adult will blow them away.

Beyond all this, destruction can be positive. Sometimes the weeds need to be whacked back to let the good stuff grow. Part of us must die so the best of us can live. Deities of destruction can do this for us.

This is not easy, nor is it safe. The fire that burns away brush can get out of control and destroy the forest. It has become fashionable in neo-Paganism to worship "dark" deities—Kali, Loki, Hecate, etc. They are seen as misunderstood. They are in fact misunderstood, but by those who see them as "fun." They are not fun. They are scary, dangerous, and difficult to deal with.

I hesitated, therefore, to include any prayers to this kind of deity. No sense in calling up trouble for people, and I have a responsibility for the use of every prayer in this book.

Yet something kept bringing me back to the need for this kind of prayer. We need to acknowledge the darker side of things in order to fill out our relationship with the universe. I compromised—a few prayers to show how they should be done and the explanation above. Not enough to rid me of responsibility, perhaps, but a slight salve to my conscience.

Hekate

Keeper of Ravenous Dogs,
Bitch Goddess,
Howler,
Bearer of Torch and Knife,
Ruler of the Dark Moon:
Hekate, I pray to you.
Turn your slaying glance from me
and direct it toward my enemies.
And if you can't turn it away,
may it be because there is something in me that must
die.
Act with wisdom and discernment, destroying only
what must go,
and giving me strength to endure the burning.

Loki

When the gods grew too comfortable in their
unending life,
you stole the apples that kept them young and made
them face age.

When they sought to cheat the giant of the wages for
*   his work,*
they turned to you to save themselves.
When Thor grew too sure of his strength to kill
Chaos, you showed him that craftiness is as
*   necessary as raw power.*
Loki, god of unpleasant truths, open my eyes to my
*   own limits.*
It is only by seeing them that I can overcome
them.[9]

$$\mathcal{D} \; \bigcirc \; \mathcal{C}$$

Fire of offering, you burn the sacrifice,
making it fit for the gods.
Burn away all my weaknesses,
making me fit for the gods.

[This prayer is good for lighting a fire, either for meditation or the beginning of a larger ritual. It should, of course, be accompanied by an offering.]

Blessings

A blessing expresses a wish that a deity look kindly on a person other than the one praying. It differs from the usual prayer in that the pray-er offers themselves up as a link between the deity and the person blessed. They stand in, as it were, for the deity, serving as a mediator.

Enter [my/our] home, and find your own,
for the old ways are kept here
and hospitality is a law all are proud to honor.[10]

Blessing for the First Day of School

Ogmios, Rosmerta, Cernunnos

> *Ogmios be at your right hand, guiding your way.*
> *Rosmerta be at your left hand, guiding your way.*
> *Cernunnos open your mind, and the Mothers keep*
> *   you safe,*
> *as you begin the great adventure of school.*

Blessings for a Child Leaving Home

> *I stand here as your father, in the place of the Father*
> *   of All,*
> *as you prepare to move away and start your own*
> *   household.*
> *Though you may live in another house, still the gods*
> *   will protect you.*
> *Though you may join your life to another's family,*
> *   still will the Ancestors guide you.*
> *Though you may travel in strange lands, still will the*
> *   spirits there welcome you.*
> *For my father's blessing is not for your ears alone:*
> *the numinous beings hear, and they will honor it.*

☽ ○ ☾

> *Go on your way in safety,*
> *bringing with you the blessings of my household gods.*
> *As you have been with us, so will you stay a part of us.*
> *May they watch over you until we meet again.*

We stand in your place, Ancestors.
We perform your deeds, Ancestors.
Do not forget, do not forget,
Let it be these words, Holy Ones,
that my heart sings in my chest.
Do not forget, do not forget,
to walk in the sacred way.
Do not forget, do not forget,
that all I see is sacred.
Do not forget, do not forget,
my sacred duty to the world which surrounds me.
Do not forget, do not forget.
Grant me this gift, you whom I worship,
not to forget.

TABLE OF OFFERINGS

Different types of spiritual entities prefer different types of offerings. If you are working with a particular named deity or spirit, you will need to research just what that deity prefers. This table, however, is a good start, especially when working with the unnamed spirits likely to be encountered.

Spiritual Entity	Food	Drink	Incense	Other
Nature Spirits	cornmeal, bread, grain, fruit, cheese	beer	sage	tobacco, quartz, pebbles
House Spirits	bread, salt, oil, fruit	milk, wine, beer	frankincense, rosemary	
Hearth Guardians	bread, butter, oil	milk	pine, rosemary	
Threshold Guardians	barley, bread	wine	juniper	
Border Guardians	eggs, honey, cakes	milk, wine, beer	rosemary, thyme, juniper	flower garlands
Garden Spirits	bread, fruit, honey, cornmeal	water, milk	bay	flowers
Deities in general	bread	wine, beer, milk	frankincense	
Birth Goddesses	bread, eggs, cookies	milk, breast milk	sandalwood, mint, rose	infant's hair, umbilical cord
Ancestor Spirits	food from the family table	drink from the family table	caraway	hair

GLOSSARY OF DEITIES

Agni ("Fire"): Vedic god of fire; the priest of the gods.

Amaterasu ("Shining in Heaven"): The Shinto Sun goddess. It is said that once she hid in a cave and plunged the world into darkness. To coax her out, the other gods put a mirror in front of the cave, and one of them began a lewd dance. Out of curiosity, she peeked out and saw her blazing reflection in the mirror. Entranced, she came out of the cave to see better. Because of this, her symbol is a mirror.

Andraste: A British war goddess favored by the famous queen Boudicca.

Anna: The Proto-Indo-European word for "old woman, grandmother." I use it in this book as a name for the Crone (the waning moon). It became the childhood word "Nana," for "grandmother." It is a nice name for the hag goddess, almost a euphemism, as if by using such a pleasant name, we might keep away the fearsome side of her.

Apollo: Greek and Roman god of music, truth, and healing.

Asklepios: The Greek god (his Roman equivalent is Aesculapius) of healing.

Athena ("Goddess of Athens?"): Greek goddess of wisdom and crafts, especially weaving.

Aurora ("Rising"): Roman dawn goddess.

Ba'al ("Lord"): Phoenician chief deity."

Boand ("White Cow," or perhaps "Giver of Cows"): The goddess of the river Boyne in Ireland. She unwittingly let loose the fiery water from the well of her husband, Nechtan. Since this was the water that inspired poets, she may be prayed to for inspiration.

Brighid ("Exalted"): Gaelic goddess of fire; the fire of inspiration, the smith, and the body (and thus of health). And, of course, that most important of fires, the hearth fire.

Cernunnos ("Antlered God"): A Gaulish deity who sits between opposites; also a god of prosperity (since merchants are those who go between). The name "Cernunnos" is sometimes used for the Wiccan God.

Charon: Greek ferryman who carries the souls of the dead across the river Styx to the Underworld.

Coyote: American Indian Trickster figure. He plays a lot of practical jokes, and a lot of practical jokes are played on him, but he is the giver of useful skills to humanity.

Daghda Mor ("Great Good God"): Not good in a moral sense, but good at things. His title "Eochu Ollathair" means "Stallion All Father," so he was most likely a chief god, but one who is presented in a rather comical sense, with a tunic that doesn't really cover his rump, and as a glutton. He mated with the Morrígain, the war goddess, at Samhain (Halloween).

Demeter: The Greek Earth goddess. Probably the most famous Greek myth tells how Demeter's daughter, Persephone, was stolen by Hades, god of the dead. Demeter mourned, and the Earth, deprived of her power, started to die. Nothing grew, and mankind was on the verge of starvation. Finally, Zeus made a deal with Demeter. Persephone could return only if she had eaten nothing in the land of the dead. Unfortunately, she had eaten a few pomegranate seeds. From then on, she was required to spend a certain amount of time each year in the dark land as its queen. During that time, Demeter mourns again, bringing on winter. When Persephone returns, however, so does life in this world, in the form of spring.

Diana: Roman goddess of the moon and the hunt; protector of children.

Dionysos: Greek god of wine, ecstasy, and devoted love.

Dyéus Ptér ("Shining Sky Father"): The Proto-Indo-European god of the bright sky and the order of the universe, king of the gods. The names "Zeus" and "Jupiter" are descended from this, and may be substituted in prayers.

Eos ("Rising"): The Greek dawn goddess. She is envisaged as a young woman dressed in the colors of dawn.

Eostre ("Rising"): An Anglo-Saxon goddess of spring and the dawn.

Epona ("Horse Goddess"): Gaulish protector of horses and cavalry; possibly goddess of sovereignty and protector of children.

Eris ("Strife, Discord"): Greek goddess of chaos and disruption.

Flora ("Flower"): The Roman goddess of flowers.

Fortuna: The Roman goddess of luck. Her emblem was the wheel, which is, of course, the wheel of fortune.

Gaṇeśa (sometimes spelled "Ganesha," and pronounced roughly that way; "Lord of Multitudes"); Gaṇapati ("Lord Gaṇeśa"): A popular Hindu god who brings fortune by removing obstacles to happiness. It makes sense that he does that, since he is in the form of an elephant, or a man with an elephant's head. Who can stand in his way?

Guan Yin (sometimes spelled "Kwan Yin;" "Perceiver of Prayers"): A Chinese goddess of mercy and compassion. Technically, she is a boddhisattva, a human being who has refused to enter into Nirvana so that she can stay behind and help everyone else. She is, nonetheless, treated like a goddess.

Gwouwindā ("Provider of Cows"): Proto-Indo-European goddess of prosperity; a mother goddess.

Gwydion ("Born of Wood(s)?"): A magician in Welsh literature who may have been a god.

Hathor ("House of Horus"): An Egyptian protective goddess often seen as a cow.

Hekate: Greek goddess of witchcraft and the crossroads.

Hera: The Roman queen of the gods; patron of marriage and children.

Inanna: Sumerian queen of the gods; she descended into the land of the dead in search of her dead husband.

Indra ("Hero?"): Vedic hero and storm god; with his lightning weapon, he killed the great serpent of chaos.

Isis ("Throne?"): Egyptian and Roman mother and protecting goddess. Her symbol was the throne. Since she protected the king, she is a good goddess to pray to for government. Her most famous myth tells how her husband, Osiris, was killed and chopped into pieces. She gathered the pieces together and revived him magically.

Janus ("Going?"): The Roman god of thresholds, doors, and beginnings.

Juno: The Roman equivalent of Hera.

Jupiter ("Shining Sky Father"): Roman king of the gods, wielder of the thunderbolt, and enforcer of justice.

Kali ("Dark"): Hindu goddess of destruction. She also has a motherly side, but to find it, you have to deal with her scary side.

Liberty: Throughout the history of the United States, Liberty has been called upon as the country's protecting goddess. Her image is found on coins and she has been celebrated in song. Her most famous image, the one seen by immigrants entering New York harbor, has become the symbol of the dreams of our country. She is thought of more as a metaphor than as an actual goddess, of course, but, as Pagans, we can invoke her in a literal way, just as the Romans did, under the name Libertas.

Loki: A figure in Norse mythology who spends most of his time working against the gods. Indeed, in the final battle at the end of the world, he will be one of the leaders of the army opposing the gods. There is no evidence that he was ever worshipped.

Lugh: Irish god of skills. One of his titles is Lamfhada ("Long-Armed," pronounced "Lah-wah-duh"). Another is "Samildanach" ("Possessing Many Arts," pronounced "Sah-vill-dah-nakh"). This reflects his many skills. A delightful story is told of him coming to the court at Tara. Those inside were feasting, and it was a rule that no one could come in during a feast, unless he had a skill no one else present had. Lugh went through his abilities—as wright, smith, champion, harpist, healer, etc. The guard at the gate told him that there was someone there in the hall already who had each of these skills. Finally, Lugh asked, "Is there anyone in there who possesses all of these skills?" and they had to let him in.

Ma'at ("Truth, Cosmic Order"): The Egyptian goddess of justice, in the sense of the way things should be. When a person dies, their soul is weighed against her feather to see if the person has done that which was right. If they have, their soul balances the feather.

Manannán mac Lir ("Little one of the island of Man, son of the sea"): Irish god of the sea, who brings us into the realm of the gods.

Marduk ("Young Bull of the Sungod Utu"): Babylonian hero god who ordered the universe.

Mari: Proto-Indo-European for "maiden," used here as a title for that aspect of the triple goddess.

Mars: Roman god of war and agriculture.

Mater: Proto-Indo-European for "mother," used here as a title for that aspect of the triple goddess.

Mater Dea: Roman; the name means "mother goddess."

The Matronae ("Mothers"): Celto-Germanic deities who appear in groups of three on a large number of images from Britian, Gaul, and Germany. They are often shown with babies, and seem to have been protectors of children.

Mḗnōts ("Measurer"): The Proto-Indo-European word for "Moon." It is a good name for a Moon god.

Mercury: Roman god of commerce and travelers.

Mithra ("Contract"): Iranian god (Vedic Mitra) of justice, friendship, and truth.

Morrígan ("Phantom Queen;" accent on the second syllable): Irish war goddess.

Nuit: The Thelemic goddess of the stars, infinite space, and infinite possibility.

Nut ("Sky"): Egyptian sky goddess, particularly the night sky.

Oghma: Irish deity of learning and eloquence.

Ogmios: The Gaulish version of Oghma.

Osiris: Egyptian Lord of the Underworld, husband of Isis. One version of his original name is Asar.

Pan ("Protector"): Greek god of the pastures.

Pele: The Hawaiian volcano goddess.

Perkunas ("Striker"): Baltic hero god, protector of the common people.

Persephone: The Greek queen of the land of the dead. (See Demeter.)

Poseidon: Greek god of the sea, the one who causes earthquakes.

Quetzacoatl ("Feathered Serpent"): Aztec wind, Sun, and creator god; a culture hero who, after giving the Aztecs corn and the practical arts, left, with a promise to return.

Rhiannon ("Great Queen): Welsh horse goddess.

Rosmerta ("Great Provider"): Gaulish god identified by the Romans with Fortuna, often represented holding a rudder, thus guiding us in our actions.

Rudra ("Howler"): Vedic god of the jungle, and not in the nice sense.

Sarasvati (also spelled "Saraswati;" "Marshy?"): A Hindu river goddess who is also a deity of words, both written and spoken.

Spider Woman: Plains and southwestern Indian culture hero.

Sūrya ("Sun"): Vedic sun god.

Taranis ("Thunder"): Gaulish thunder god.

Terminus ("Border"): The Roman god of the borders (as in "terminate"). Like border deities in many cultures, his images are the border stones. If possible, erect one large stone or several small stones at each corner of your property to represent him. You may even find surveyors' markers there. These are your images of Terminus, and that is where you should make offerings to him.

Thor ("Thunder"): Norse god of thunderstorms; he protects his worshippers with Mjølnir, the hammer he throws.

Thoth: Egyptian god of wisdom, magic, and writing; he is pictured with the head of an ibis.

Uṣas (Rising;" also spelled "Ushas"): The Vedic dawn goddess.

Viṣṇu (also spelled "Vishnu"): The Vedic god who, by taking three steps, extended the universe to its current size.

Woden ("Rager, Mad One"): Anglo-Saxon god (cognate with the Norse Odin) of magic, wisdom, and war; also a guide to travelers.

Venus ("Desire"): Roman goddess of love and beauty.

Vesta ("Burning?"): The hearth goddess of Rome. She was believed to be present in the fire on the hearth, where she was given some of the food from each day's main meal.

Yama ("Twin"): The Vedic god of death.

Zeus ("Shining Sky"): Greek king of the gods.

Zurvan Akarana "Time who is Alone"): The god of eternal time in a heretical form of Zoroastrianism.

— B —

— C —

— D —

— G —

— H —

— I —

— M —

— T —

— Y —

— Z —

ANNOTATED BIBLIOGRAPHY

Austen, Hallie Iglehart. *The Heart of the Goddess.* Berkeley, CA: Wingbow Press, 1990. Contains some very beautiful goddess images that might spark an interest in a particular deity; the images can be used in a shrine. The text, unfortunately, is riddled with errors, and should not be trusted.

Benveniste, Emile. *Indo-European Language and Society.* trans. Elizabeth Palmer. Coral Gables, FL: University of Miami Press, 1969.

Boyce Mary, ed. and trans. *Textual Sources for the Study of Zoroastrianism.* Chicago: University of Chicago Press, 1984.

Carmichael, Alexander, ed. and trans. *Carmina Gadelica.* Hudson, NY: Lindisfarne Press, 1992. Scottish prayers collected around the end of the 19th century. There is some question as to just how authentic they are, but they are beautifully written and can act as good models for your own writing.

Dumezil, George. *Archaic Roman Religion*, 2 vol. trans. Philip Krapp. Baltimore, MD: Johns Hopkins University Press, 1996 (1966).

Eliade, Mircea, ed. *Essential Sacred Writings from Around the World.* San Francisco: HarperSanFrancisco, 1967. This contains many prayers, as well as excerpts from scriptures.

Evelyn-White, Hugh G., ed. and trans. *Hesiod, Homeric Hymns, Epic Cycle, Homerica.* Cambridge, MA: Harvard University Press, 1936 (1914). Besides being a major source of information on Greek mythology, the Homeric Hymns are beautiful prayers.

Gantz, Jeffrey, trans. *The Mabinogion.* New York: Penguin Books, 1976.

Grant, Frederick C., ed. *Ancient Roman Religion.* New York: Liberal Arts Press, 1957. Roman texts, including prayers.

Grant, Michael, and Rachel Kitzinger. *Civilization of the Ancient Mediterranean: Greece and Rome,* vol. II. New York: Charles Scribner's Sons, 1988.

Graves, Robert. *The White Goddess.* New York: Farrar, Straus, and Giroux, 1948. Just don't believe a word it says and you'll be alright.

Heiler, Friedrich. *Prayer: A Study in the History and Psychology of Religion.* Ed. and trans. by Samuel McComb. New York: Oxford University Press, 1932.

Jackson, Kenneth Hurlstone, ed. and trans. *A Celtic Miscellany.* Harmondsworth, UK: Penguin Classics, 1975. A collection of Celtic tales and poems.

Lincoln, Bruce. *Death, War, and Sacrifice: Studies in Ideology and Practice.* Chicago: University of Chicago Press, 1991.

Lyle, Emily B. "Dumezil's Three Functions and Indo-European Cosmic Structure." *History of Religions,* 22:1 (Aug 1982), pp. 25-44.

MacMullen, Ramsay. *Paganism in the Roman Empire.* New Haven, CT: Yale University Press, 1981.

Marcus Aurelius. *Meditations.* trans. Maxwell Staniforth. Harmondsworth, UK: Penguin Classics, 1964.

O'Flaherty, Wendy Doniger, ed. and trans. *The Rig Veda.* London: Penguin Books, 1981. The oldest of the Vedic prayers. Good inspiration and useful as examples.

Ovid. *The Metamorphoses.* trans. Horace Gregory. New York: Penguin Books, 1960. Collection of Greek and Roman myths.

Poetic Edda. trans. Lee M. Hollander. Austin, TX: University of Texas Press, 1962. One of our major sources of information on Norse religion. Hollander limits himself to words with Germanic roots, which makes the poems sometimes difficult to understand, but still beautiful.

Polomé, Edgar C. "Old Norse Religious Terminology in Indo-European Perspective," in *Language, Society, and Paleoculture: Essays by Edgar C. Polome.* Selected and introduced by Anwar S. Dil. Stanford, CA: Stanford University Press, 1982.

Roberts, Elizabeth and Elias Amidon, eds. *Earth Prayers from Around the World: 365 Prayers, Poems, and Invocations Honoring the Earth.* San Francisco: HarperSanFrancisco, 1991. Prayers from many religions, all roughly associated with what might be called "Earth spirituality."

Sturlusson, Snorri. *Edda.* trans. Anthony Faulkes. Rutland, VT: Charles E. Tuttle, 1987.

Virgil. *The Aeneid.* trans. Allan Mandelbaum. New York: Bantam Books, 1981.

Watts, Alan. *The Way of Zen.* New York: Vintage Books, 1957.

NOTES

Chapter 3:

1 The individual flames are imagined to be tongues, each of which can carry the offerer's message; the fire joins you in praying.

Chapter 5:

1 By "race" I do not mean black or white, but "species." I use the word simply because "race" scans better than "species," and sounds less scientific and more emotional.

Chapter 6:

1 This prayer can be said before any other prayer or at the beginning of any ritual. Who is the gatekeeper? He is the god (and in most traditions, this deity is male) who holds the gate between the world of gods and the human world. Examples are Hermes, Manannan, Agni, and Cernunnos.

Chapter 7:

1 Although Wicca does not practice literal sacrifice, it does have a sacrificial theology. The God is not only

the lord of all life; he is also the one who dies with the year, who is cut down in the fall, to reign in the Otherworld as Lord of Death. As such, he is the first sacrifice. The line "worthy of sacrifice" is thus, as I said earlier, ambiguous, meaning both "worthy to receive sacrifice," and "worthy to be offered in sacrifice." The animals with which he is identified in this prayer are the four animals assigned by the Indo-Europeans to the four directions, starting in the east with the bull and moving clockwise. They were also the animals most desirous as sacrificial offerings. This prayer may also be used as a litany.

2 The cosmos envisioned in this prayer is similar to that of Norse tradition, with the cosmic tree at the center of the universe fed from the well of Mimir at its feet. I have changed the Norse ash to an oak because I prefer oak, but the other differences are a result of the duotheism of Wicca. The well becomes the Goddess herself, but its role both as the source of the tree's nourishment and the pattern it gives to existence (its wyrd) has not been changed. This prayer could equally well have been placed in the chapter on petitionary prayers, but the majority of it is praise, so I have included it here.

3 This prayer refers to the legend of the descent of the Goddess in Gardnerian Wicca, in which the Goddess goes to the land of the dead and confronts the god of the dead. She then becomes queen of that land, and brings rebirth to its inhabitants. This prayer is especially appropriate for times of despair. It could, for instance, be recited at a funeral. The Goddess brought

rebirth to the spirits in the Otherworld; she will bring it to us. She, herself, went through darkness; she will bring us through it as well.

4 This prayer to the god of storms contains imagery from several traditions. There is Mjølnir, the axe of Thor ("thunder"), which returns to his hand when it is thrown so he can throw it again. I've included several aspects of the Vedic Indra; the bull scattering seed (rain), the combination of fire and water (lightning and rain), and the description of this god as a wild beast. The prayer may be used for any storm god, however, such as the Canaanite Ba'al ("Lord") or Gaulish Taranis ("Thunder"). The last line reflects the old belief that the spring's thunderstorms fertilize the fields. This prayer may, therefore, be used as a prayer for rain in spring.

Chapter 8:

1 This can be used to consecrate a Goddess image, passing it from hand to hand as each person calls out a title.

Chapter 10:

1 From a Wiccan point of view, "She" is the Goddess, and the Sun is an image of the God. From a more polytheistic point of view, "She" is the goddess of dawn.

2 Both ship and wagon are seen, in different cultures and sometimes both in one, as the vehicles that carry the Sun through the sky. There is no reason to see these as

contradicting each other; Paganism has room for many images.

Chapter II:

1 When the Sun sets, the New Moon emerges from his brightness, where she has hidden all day. She is a maiden, but also erotic; the flowers she scatters may be symbolic either of general fertility or sexuality. She appears out of the darkness as well, out of the three dark nights of the Moon. She is a pruning sickle, because her erotic nature is slightly dangerous in so far as it is not in the service of the community. It is raw power, not yet controlled. Nevertheless, it encourages growth.

2 "Mirrors" is meant both literally, since the image of the Moon appears in the pool as it would in a mirror, and figuratively, in the sense that the pool is a symbol of the Moon, round and shining. The same symbolism is found in the next prayer.

3 The waning crescent Moon, as the symbol of the Crone, is likened to a harvesting sickle. It rises just before sunrise and is soon blotted out by the brightness of the Sun. It cannot be seen, but it is still there, just as old age and death wait for us. The hope, stated in the last line, is that the sickle will bring wisdom (cutting away ignorance), but not death. Even in its function of reaping, the waning Moon brings "loving mercy." There is a Zen story that expresses this well. A student asks his master questions, but each time the master only hits him with a stick. He finally grows sick of this and goes

to another master. He tells the new master the story, but instead of giving him sympathy, the new master berates him for not appreciating the first master's "grandmotherly kindness." It is just this sort of wisdom that we seek from the Old Woman. Sometimes we need to get hit with a stick.

Chapter 12:

1 The "summer offering" is the offering up of summer itself, burned by the flaming colors of the autumn leaves. Each of the forms of life that are dying at this time are granted, by this prayer, the status of a sacrifice. This prayer is a gift to those beings who cannot, themselves pray; we pray on their behalf, giving meaning to their deaths.

Chapter 13:

1 It is never too early to learn if a deity has taken interest in your child. After this prayer, sit or stand in silence for a while, listening. It is likely that a deity will enter your awareness, thereby answering your questions. If not, continue with your life; the answer will likely come in time. You can pray this prayer as often as you need to, until you receive an answer—every day if you like. If you do not learn the child's patron before he or she is old enough to pray, the child can do it him or herself. Once the deities have made themselves known to you, make sure you make an offering to them. Install an

image of them in your family shrine and pray to them regularly. My daughter is grown and I still pray to her patron at least once a day.

2   The imagery in this prayer is based on Indo-European beliefs, in which the Lord of the Otherworld was once alive. In the first sacrifice, however, he was the victim. Through his sacrifice, the world came into being, and, as the first to die, he became the appropriate ruler of the dead. (See Bruce Lincoln's *Death, War, and Sacrifice* for a wonderful description of this myth.) I find this concept moving, so I have incorporated it into my own beliefs. It is quite compatible with most forms of Wicca, where the God is both the dying god (with overtones of sacrifice) and the lord of the dead.

Chapter 14:

1   The world of the Pagan includes more than the products of nature. The gods not only produce the natural world, they give culture. Athena, Oghma, Thoth, Coyote—in every Pagan society, there is at least one deity revered as the originator of skills and learning. To make too strong a distinction between natural and artificial would not, therefore, be the Pagan thing to do. We are, after all, ourselves part of nature, and so are our products and skills. One way to prevent these products and skills from causing excessive damage to the others with whom we share this planet is to revere the deities who gave them to us. In this way, we are made constantly aware of their sanctity and, thus, of the responsibility they demand from us.

2 This is to the Goddess, envisioned as a cow: the Egyptian Hathor, Irish Boand ("giver of cattle"), cow-eyed Hera. While being compared to a cow may not seem exactly flattering to us, it was thought to be so by the ancients. This was, of course, especially true of those people whose economy was based on cattle.

3 The Sun measures as well; in this case, the daily sky. Looking down on us all day, he is often a symbol of a god of moral judgment. He measures the sky by his passage through it and, just as this measurement is unerring, he expects ours to be as well. We are not quite so precise, however, and this prayer asks him to understand this.

4 This prayer to Asklepios is for a doctor to pray before each day's work. Only a little change would be needed for it to be used by a patient or a patient's friend.

5 This may be used to help smooth a journey, but it may also be used to help smooth a life. The way and the path are images of how things should be, and for how we should act.

6 If any situation requires prayer, it's traffic. The observation of the harm done by anger is Marcus Aurelius's.

7 Although this was written for Thor, it may be used for any deity who is conceived of as both warrior and god of thunder. Examples include Jupiter, Zeus, Indra, and Perkunas. The hammer or double-headed axe is a widespread emblem of this type of deity.

8 At the oracle of Dodona in ancient Greece, the movements of oak branches were used to determine the advice of the gods. In this prayer, it is explained that, since everything is connected with everything else, then from any one thing, any other thing may be known. Since leaves reflect the wind, they are a perfect example of this relationship and are thus a good choice for divination.

9 There is no evidence that Loki was ever worshipped. He may have existed only in myths, with the ancients knowing better than to call out to him. There was, after all, enough chaos in their lives. Still, I decided to include this prayer for two reasons. First, no matter what the ancients may have thought, neo-Pagans are going to pray to him, so they may as well pray relatively safely. Second, today our world is very ordered, and becoming more so every day. A little bit of chaos might do us some good, if it is channeled into destroying pleasant lies.

10 This blessing calls on the Pagan virtue of hospitality, one of the primary features of the sacred order of things. In saying it, a person is taking on the role of the gods themselves, and honoring them with right actions. It is a good blessing to inscribe on a plaque and hang by your door. Of course, you must live up to it.

To Our Readers

Weiser Books, an imprint of Red Wheel/Weiser, publishes books across the entire spectrum of occult, esoteric, speculative, and New Age subjects. Our mission is to publish quality books that will make a difference in people's lives without advocating any one particular path or field of study. We value the integrity, originality, and depth of knowledge of our authors.

Our readers are our most important resource, and we appreciate your input, suggestions, and ideas about what you would like to see published.

Visit our website at *www.redwheelweiser.com* to learn about our upcoming books and free downloads, and be sure to go to *www.redwheelweiser.com/newsletter* to sign up for newsletters and exclusive offers.

You can also contact us at *info@rwwbooks.com* or at

Red Wheel/Weiser, LLC
65 Parker Street, Suite 7
Newburyport, MA 01950